changes

ENGLISH FOR INTERNATIONAL COMMUNICATION

2

STUDENT'S
BOOK

Jack C. Richards

with Jonathan Hull
and Susan Proctor

CAMBRIDGE
UNIVERSITY PRESS

PUBLISHED BY THE PRESS SYNDICATE OF THE UNIVERSITY OF CAMBRIDGE
The Pitt Building, Trumpington Street, Cambridge, United Kingdom

CAMBRIDGE UNIVERSITY PRESS
The Edinburgh Building, Cambridge CB2 2RU, UK
40 West 20th Street, New York, NY 10011–4211, USA
10 Stamford Road, Oakleigh, VIC 3166, Australia
Ruiz de Alarcón 13, 28014 Madrid, Spain
Dock House, The Waterfront, Cape Town 8001, South Africa

http://www.cambridge.org

First published 1995
Sixth printing 2001

Printed in the United Kingdom at the University Press, Cambridge

ISBN 0 521 44930 8 Student's Book 2
ISBN 0 521 44936 7 Teacher's Book 2
ISBN 0 521 44933 2 Workbook 2
ISBN 0 521 44942 1 Class Cassette Set 2
ISBN 0 521 44939 1 Student Cassette 2

Contents

Plan of Book 2

Unit 1	Topics	Functions	Grammar/Pronunciation
	People; education; childhood; the past	Talking about oneself; introducing oneself; talking about someone else	**Grammar** Past simple for narration; past simple and *used to* for habitual actions **Pronunciation** Weak forms of *were* and *did*

Unit 2	Topics	Functions	Grammar/Pronunciation
	Cities; towns; buildings; directions	Talking about local landmarks; giving directions	**Grammar** Direct and indirect questions; sequence markers; imperatives **Pronunciation** Question intonation

Unit 3	Topics	Functions	Grammar/Pronunciation
	Housing; prices; towns	Describing homes, neighbourhoods, towns; describing positive and negative features; making comparisons	**Grammar** Adjectives and adverbs; comparison of adjectives **Pronunciation** Sentence stress

Units 1–3 Review

Unit 4	Topics	Functions	Grammar/Pronunciation
	Food; experiences; instructions: recipes	Describing experiences; giving instructions	**Grammar** Past simple and present perfect; two-part verbs **Pronunciation** Word stress

Unit 5	Topics	Functions	Grammar/Pronunciation
	Travel; holidays; plans	Giving advice; describing things to do in a city; describing plans	**Grammar** Modal verbs; future with present continuous and *going to* **Pronunciation** Weak form of *going to*

Unit 6	Topics	Functions	Grammar/Pronunciation
	Requests; complaints; apologies	Making requests; accepting/refusing requests; complaining; apologising; making excuses	**Grammar** Imperatives; requests with modals **Pronunciation** Weak forms of *could* and *would*

Units 4–6 Review

Unit 7	Topics	Functions	Grammar/Pronunciation
	Gadgets; machines	Describing what things are for; describing problems with things; suggesting causes for problems	**Grammar** Gerunds and infinitives; countable and uncountable nouns **Pronunciation** Stress in compound nouns

Listening	Writing/Reading	Interchange Activity
Listening for information about someone's life; choosing the correct response to questions about the past	**Writing** Writing about your childhood **Reading** The eighties; a pop group of the eighties	Class profile

Listening	Writing/Reading	Interchange Activity
Listening for places and directions	**Writing** Writing directions **Reading** Transport firsts; walking tour of Chichester	Giving directions in a city

Listening	Writing/Reading	Interchange Activity
Listening to descriptions of housing for sale or rent; choosing the correct response to questions involving comparisons	**Writing** Writing about similarities and differences **Reading** Unusual facts about cities; housing for sale	Housing survey

Listening	Writing/Reading	Interchange Activity
Listening to a discussion between a dietician and patient; identifying incorrect information in a description	**Writing** Writing a recipe **Reading** Ethnic foods; restaurant reviews	Finding out more about other students

Listening	Writing/Reading	Interchange Activity
Listening to advice about sightseeing; listening to travel plans	**Writing** Writing an itinerary **Reading** Travel facts; fitness in the air	Planning a holiday

Listening	Writing/Reading	Interchange Activity
Listening to requests and choosing the correct response; listening to complaints and excuses	**Writing** Writing a letter to a newspaper **Reading** Complaints; letters to the editor	Making complaints and making excuses

Listening	Writing/Reading	Interchange Activity
Listening to descriptions of gadgets; listening to problems with gadgets	**Writing** Writing a note describing a problem **Reading** Important inventions; advertisements for gadgets	Returning something to a shop

Unit 8	Topics	Functions	Grammar/Pronunciation
	Holidays; festivals; customs	Describing holidays, festivals, customs and special events	**Grammar** Relative clauses of time; adverbial clauses of time **Pronunciation** Stress and rhythm in sentences

Unit 9	Topics	Functions	Grammar/Pronunciation
	Life in the past, present and future; changes and contrasts	Comparing time periods; describing possibilities	**Grammar** Past and present tenses; future with *will* and *may*; 1st and 2nd conditionals with modals **Pronunciation** Pitch

Units 7–9 Review

Unit 10	Topics	Functions	Grammar/Pronunciation
	People's abilities, skills, and qualities; jobs	Describing abilities and skills; describing people's qualities	**Grammar** Responses with *so* and *neither*; adjectives and adverbs **Pronunciation** Stress in responses

Unit 11	Topics	Functions	Grammar/Pronunciation
	Buildings; landmarks; world knowledge	Describing buildings and landmarks; describing people's characteristics	**Grammar** Past simple passive with *by*; present simple passive without *by* **Pronunciation** Linked sounds

Unit 12	Topics	Functions	Grammar/Pronunciation
	Information about someone's past	Talking and asking about things people have been doing; talking and asking about past events	**Grammar** Past simple, past continuous, present perfect continuous; adverbial clauses and phrases **Pronunciation** Sentence stress

Units 10–12 Review

Unit 13	Topics	Functions	Grammar/Pronunciation
	Films and books; interests; entertainers	Describing films, books and people	**Grammar** Past and present participles; relative clauses **Pronunciation** Word stress

Unit 14	Topics	Functions	Grammar/Pronunciation
	Meanings; proverbs; excuses	Giving definitions and explaining meanings; reporting what people say	**Grammar** Modals and adverbs; reported speech **Pronunciation** Sentence stress for information focus

Unit 15	Topics	Functions	Grammar/Pronunciation
	Money; hopes; suggestions; speculations; predicaments	Speculating about the future and the past; talking about predicaments	**Grammar** 2nd and 3rd conditionals with modals; past modals **Pronunciation** Weak form of *have*

Units 13–15 Review

Interchange Activities

Listening	Writing/Reading	Interchange Activity
Listening to descriptions of special days and customs	**Writing** Writing about a birthday **Reading** Holidays and festivals; unusual customs	Finding out how people celebrate special days and times
Listening for references to past, present and future; listening to complaints and possible solutions	**Writing** Writing about hopes for the future **Reading** Opinion poll about the past, present and future; unusual laws	Finding out people's opinions
Listening to statements and choosing a correct response; listening for positive or negative opinions	**Writing** Writing about the family **Reading** Facts about the world of work; horoscopes	Describing work, skills and abilities
Listening for specific facts about landmarks; listening for facts about a country	**Writing** Writing about a country **Reading** Famous landmarks; the Czech Republic	Culture quiz
Listening for references to the past and present and choosing the correct response; listening to facts about a person's life	**Writing** Writing a biography **Reading** Some facts about celebrities; story of a musician	Conducting an interview
Listening to descriptions of books and films	**Writing** Writing a film review **Reading** Ten top films; film reviews	Film quiz
Listening for excuses; listening for telephone messages	**Writing** Writing telephone messages **Reading** Languages; the truth about lying	Finding out about likes, dislikes and wishes
Listening to advice and suggestions; listening to problems on a radio show	**Writing** Writing to an advice columnist **Reading** Record breaking events; newspaper advice column	Talking about hypothetical predicaments

Introduction

Changes is a three-level course in English as a foreign language for young adults and adults. The course covers the skills of listening, speaking, reading, and writing, with particular emphasis on listening and speaking. The primary goal of the course is to teach communicative competence – that is, the ability to communicate in English according to the situation, purpose, and roles of the participants. It is adapted from *Interchange*, the highly successful course by the same authors. Whereas *Interchange* is based on American English, *Changes* presents a British English model for international communication. Level Two takes students from low intermediate to intermediate level.

Course length

Changes is a self-contained course covering all four language skills. Each level covers between 90 and 120 hours of class instruction time. Depending on how the book is used, however, more or less time may be used. The Teacher's Book gives detailed suggestions for optional activities to extend each unit. Where less time is available, the course can be taught in approximately 90 hours by reducing the amount of time spent on Interchange Activities, reading, writing, optional activities, and the Workbook.

Course components

Student's Book The Student's Book contains fifteen units, with a review unit after every three units. There are five review units in all. Following Unit 15, there is a set of communication activities called Interchange Activities, one for each unit of the book. Unit summaries, at the end of each unit, contain lists of the key vocabulary and expressions used in the unit as well as grammar summaries.

Teacher's Book A separate Teacher's Book contains detailed suggestions on how to teach the course, lesson-by-lesson notes, an extensive set of optional follow-up activities, complete answer keys to the Student's Book and Workbook exercises, tests for use in class and test answer keys, and transcripts of those listening activities not printed in the Student's Book and in the five tests. The tests can be photocopied and given to students after each review unit is completed.

Workbook The Workbook contains stimulating and varied exercises that provide additional practice on the teaching points presented in the Student's Book. A variety of exercise types is used to develop students' skills in grammar, reading, writing, spelling, vocabulary, and pronunciation. The Workbook can be used for classwork and for homework.

Class Cassettes A set of two cassettes for class use accompanies the Student's Book. The cassettes contain recordings of the conversations, grammar focus summaries, pronunciation exercises, and listening activities, as well as recordings of the listening exercises used in the tests. A variety of native-speaker voices and accents is used, as well as some non-native speakers of English. Exercises that are recorded on the cassettes are indicated with the symbol ▭ .

Student Cassette A cassette is also available for students to use for self-study. The Student Cassette contains selected recordings of conversations, grammar, and pronunciation exercises from the Student's Book.

Approach and methodology

Changes teaches students to use English for everyday situations and purposes related to work, school, social life, and leisure. The underlying philosophy of the course is that learning a foreign language is more rewarding, meaningful, and effective when the language is used for authentic communication. Information-sharing activities provide a maximum amount of student-generated communication. Throughout *Changes*, students have the opportunity to personalise the language they learn and make use of their own life experience and world knowledge.

The course has the following key features:

Integrated Syllabus *Changes* has an integrated, multi-skills syllabus that links grammar and communicative functions. The course recognises grammar as an essential component of foreign language proficiency. However, it presents grammar communicatively, with controlled accuracy-based activities leading to fluency-based communicative practice. The syllabus also contains the four skills of listening, speaking, reading, and writing, as well as pronunciation and vocabulary.

Adult and International Content *Changes* deals with contemporary topics that are of high interest and relevance to both students and teachers. Each unit includes real-world information on a variety of topics.

Enjoyable and Useful Learning Activities A wide variety of interesting and enjoyable activities forms the basis for each unit. The course makes extensive use of pair work, small group activities, role plays, and information-sharing activities. Practice exercises allow for a maximum amount of individual student practice and enable learners to personalise and apply the language they learn. Throughout the course, natural and useful language is presented that can be used in real-life situations.

What each unit contains

Each unit in *Changes* contains the following kinds of exercises:

Snapshot The Snapshots contain interesting information about the world, introduce the topic of the unit or part of the unit, and also develop vocabulary. Either the teacher can present these exercises in class as reading or discussion activities, or students can read them by themselves in class or for homework, using their dictionaries if necessary.

Conversation The Conversations introduce the new grammar of each unit in a communicative context and also present functions and conversational expressions. The teacher can either present the conversations with the Class Cassette or read the dialogues aloud.

Pronunciation These exercises focus on important features of spoken English, including stress, rhythm, intonation, contractions, and sound contrasts.

Grammar focus The new grammar of each unit is presented in colour panels and is followed by practice activities that move from controlled to freer practice. These activities always give students a chance to use the grammar they have learned for real communication.

Listening The listening activities develop a wide variety of listening skills, including listening for gist, listening for details, and inferring meaning from context. These exercises often require completing an authentic task while listening, such as taking telephone messages. The recordings on the Class Cassettes contain both scripted and unscripted conversations with natural pauses, hesitations, and interruptions that occur in real speech.

Word power The Word power activities develop students' vocabulary through a variety of interesting tasks, such as word maps.

Writing The writing exercises include practical writing tasks that extend and reinforce the teaching points in the unit and help develop students' composition skills. The Teacher's Book shows how to use these exercises to focus on the process of writing.

Reading The reading passages develop a variety of reading skills, including guessing words from context, skimming, scanning, and making inferences. Various text types adapted from authentic sources are used.

Interchange Activities The Interchange Activities are pair work and group work tasks, information-sharing tasks, and role plays that encourage real communication. These exercises are a central part of the course and allow students to extend and personalise what they have learned in each unit.

From the Authors

We hope that you will like using *Changes* and find it useful, interesting, and fun. Our goal has been to provide teachers and students with activities that make the English class a time to look forward to and, at the same time, provide students with the skills they need to use English outside the classroom. Please let us know how you enjoyed it and good luck!

Jack C. Richards
Jonathan Hull
Susan Proctor

Where were you?

Greetings	*I'm from …; I'm studying …*
Talking about yourself	*I went …; I used to go …*
Talking about memories	

1 Conversation: Greetings and introductions

1 Listen.

Maria: Hello. Can I give you a hand?
Karen: Oh, thanks.
Maria: I'm Maria, by the way. I'm in Room 203.
Karen: Oh! I'm moving into 204.
My name's Karen.
Maria: Nice to meet you.
Karen: Nice to meet you, too.
Maria: Where are you from, Karen?
Karen: Well, I was born in Stuttgart,
but I live in Bristol now.
Maria: Oh, really? And what are
you studying?
Karen: I'm studying history and
economics. And what about you,
Maria? What are you studying?
Maria: I'm studying French and German.
This is my second year. Listen, why
don't you come over for coffee later?
Karen: Thanks, I'd love to.

2 *Pair work*

Practise the conversation. Use your own information and these expressions.

Good morning/afternoon/evening.	What's your name/surname?	Nice to meet you.
Hello/Hi!	My name's …	Where are you from?
		I'm from …
		I was born in …

2 Teacher's turn

Ask your teacher these questions.

Where are you from?
Where did you live as a child?
What did you study?
What languages do you speak?
Where do you live now?

Now think of three more questions and ask them.

3 Grammar focus: Past simple 🔲

> **Was** Karen born in Bristol?   **Did** Karen **live** in Stuttgart as a child?
> No, she **wasn't**. /(Yes, she **was**.)   No, she **didn't**./(Yes, she **did**.)
> She **wasn't** born in Bristol.   She **didn't live** in Stuttgart.
> Where **was** she born?   Where **did** she **live**?
> She **was** born in Stuttgart.   She **lived** in Bristol and **went** to school there.

1 Complete the conversation. Then read it with a partner.

A: Could you tell me a little about yourself? Where were you born?
B: I .... in ....
A: Oh? .... live there as a child, too?
B: Yes, ... / No, ... I .... in ....
A: Where .... go to school?
B: I .... to school in ....

2 Now write five questions to ask other students.
Use the past simple and these words.

Where …?
When …?
Why …?
What …?
Which …?

4 Pronunciation: Weak forms with *were you* and *did you* 🔲

1 Listen to the weak forms in these questions.

Where **were you** born?   Where **did you** live as a child?   **Did you** go to university?

2 Now listen and practise these questions.

Where were you born?   Did you go to university?
Where did you go to school?   When were you there?
Did you study English at school?   What did you study there?

3 *Pair work*

Now ask another student the questions you wrote in Exercise 3.2. Use the weak forms.

5 Listening 📼

1 Look at these questions and write down
your answers.

What is your idea of perfect happiness?
When and where were you happiest?
What or who is your greatest love?
What is your greatest fear?
Which talent would you most like to have?
What is your greatest regret?

2 Now listen to the answers the actor Jean-Claude
Van Damme gave to these questions and some others.
His answers are spoken by an actor.

Are any of his answers similar to yours?

6 Interview

1 Make a list of three of the questions above and three questions of your own.

2 *Pair work*

Now ask your partner your questions and make notes of her/his answers.

3 *Class activity*

Tell the class something interesting about your partner.

7 Word power: Verbs

1 *Pair work*

Match the verbs in List A with their opposites in List B.

A   B

a ask   f send   .... answer   .... hate
b give   g sell   .... buy   .... receive
c go   h sit   .... come   .... lose
d love   i start   .... finish   .... stand
e remember   j win   .... forget   .... take

2 Now write down the past simple forms of the verbs above. Compare with a partner.
Then use six of the verbs in sentences as in this example.

When I was at school I loved maths, but I hated English.

8 Snapshot

THE 80s

1980
Ronald Reagan was elected
President of the United States

1981
Prince Charles of Britain
married Lady Diana Spencer

1982
Italy's football team won
the World Cup

1983
The US Senate agreed to make
Martin Luther King's birthday
a national holiday

1984
Indira Gandhi
was assassinated

1989
East Germany opened
the Berlin Wall

1988
Australia celebrated its
200th birthday

1987
Van Gogh's painting *Sunflowers*
sold for £26.5 million

1986
Spain and Portugal joined
the European Community

1985
Mikhail Gorbachev became
the leader of the USSR

Discussion

Can you think of any other important world events that happened in the eighties?
What is the most important thing that happened to you in the eighties?

9 Conversation

1   Listen.

Anne: I watched a great video last night –
           Stand by me.
Jeff: Oh, yes. I loved that film.
           It really reminded me of my childhood.
Claudio: Me too! What's your favourite
           childhood memory, Jeff?
Jeff: Um, let me see. Oh, I remember!
           My best friend and I built a tree house
           in the back garden one summer.
           We used to play in it every day
           after school. It was great fun!

2   Now listen to the rest of the conversation
    and take notes about Anne's and Claudio's
    favourite childhood memories.

10 Grammar focus: *Used to* 🔲

> What games **did** you **use to** play as a child?   **Did** you **use to** have a hobby?
>
> I **used to** play chess.   Yes, I **used to** collect stamps.
>
> I **didn't use to** play tennis.

1 Complete these sentences. Then compare with a partner.

   a At school I used to …
   b For our summer holidays we used to …
   c I used to be …, but I'm not any more.
   d At weekends my friends and I used to …

2 Now write five sentences about
   yourself with *used to*.
   Then compare with a partner.

11 Memories

1 *Pair work*

Ask another student these questions about her/his childhood.

Where did you use to live as a child?   What sports did you use to play at school?
Did you use to have any hobbies?

Now ask three more questions of your own with *used to*.

2 *Class activity*

Tell the class two interesting things about your partner.

12 Listening 🔲

Listen and tick the correct response.

a .... No, I wasn't.   e .... Yes, in a restaurant.
  .... Yes, I used to.   .... No, I studied
b .... Yes, I was.   economics.
  .... No, I did French.   f .... Yes, we used to.
c .... From 1986 to 1990.   .... No, not really.
  .... In Manchester.
d .... Yes, I played football.
  .... Yes, it is.

> **INTERCHANGE 1:**
> CLASS PROFILE
>
> Discover some
> interesting facts about
> other students in
> your class.
> Turn to page 125.

13 Writing

1 Write about your childhood using the *past simple* and *used to*. Use this as a model:

> *When I was four, my family moved to Brighton. We had a small, two-storey house and a big garden. My older brother and I used to play lots of games together. Sometimes we invited other children from our street and we often made a lot of noise. My mother used to get really angry...*

2 Group work

Take turns reading your compositions and answer any questions.

14 **Reading:** Looking back from here

1 Do you know the Pet Shop Boys? Do you like their music? Read this article about them.

The Pet Shop Boys

In 1981, two young men from the north of England met in a music shop in the King's Road in London and decided to start writing songs together. By 1983, they had a name, two or three songs and not much else. It was in America that they recorded their first song, called *West End Girls*. This was an instant No. 1 hit when it was released in Britain in 1985. From that moment the Pet Shop Boys were on the way to world wide success.

They are popular with the fans of the Beatles and Rolling Stones of the 60s as well as the club-going children of the 90s. Perhaps they keep their fans because they sound different, but not *too* different; young, but not *too* young.

So how do they see the future? What happens to Neil Tennant and Chris Lowe if their millions of fans move on to something new? "I don't think we'd stop," says Tennant, "we'd just think the public was wrong!"

And what about their strange name? Well, back in the 80s they had friends who worked in a pet shop in London, and … well …, that's it, really. "I've always thought it was a stupid name," says Lowe. "But they were *your* friends!" says Tennant.

Stupid or not, it has made them very rich and very, very famous … and strangely, one of their albums from 1993 is called *Very Pet Shop Boys*.

2 What nationality are the Pet Shop Boys? How did they get their name?
When and where did they make their first record? Why is their music popular?

Unit summary

Grammar

1 Past simple questions: *Be*

Was I …?	Where was I …?
Were you …?	Where were you …?
Was she …?	Where was she …?
Was he …?	Where was he …?
Was it …?	Where was it …?
Were we …?	Where were we …?
Were you …?	Where were you …?
Were they …?	Where were they …?

2 Questions and statements: *Used to*

Did you **use to** collect stamps?
Yes, I **did.**
No, I **didn't use to** collect stamps.
No, I **didn't.**
No, I **never used to** collect stamps.
No, I **never did.**

3 For past tense of irregular verbs, see page 142.

Key vocabulary

Nouns
best friend
child
childhood
fear
film
football
foreign language
French
friend
fun
game
garden
German
happiness
history
hobby
holiday
job
language
memory
primary school
regret
secondary school
singer
sports
stamps
storey
summer
surname
talent
tree house
university
video

Verbs
be
build
buy
collect
come
do
forget

get
give
go
have
leave
live
lose
love
move
play
remind
sell
send
sit
speak
stand
start
study
swim
used to
watch
win

Adjectives
favourite
great
perfect
personal

Adverbs
any more
as
here
really
there

Prepositions
from
in
to

Conjunctions
and
but
or

Titles
Mr
Mrs
Miss
Ms

Question words
What …?
When …?
Where …?
Which …?
Why …?

Expressions
Hello.
Hi!
Good morning/afternoon/evening.
Could you tell me a little about yourself?
Nice to meet you.
Listen …
Can I give you a hand?
Thanks.
Why don't you come over for coffee later?
I'd love to.
What about you?
Me too.
Really?

Excuse me, I'm lost!

Asking the way	*Can/Could you tell me …?*
Giving directions	*Turn right/left …*
City landmarks and facilities	*First, … then … next …*

1 Snapshot

TRANSPORT FiRSTS

1830 First passenger train service: Britain
1863 First underground railway: London
1873 First cable cars: San Francisco
1896 First taxi cabs: Stuttgart
1898 First US subway: Boston
1910 First trolley bus: Los Angeles
1952 First commercial jet: the Comet
1964 First bullet train (130 mph): Japan
1970 First jumbo jet: Boeing 747
1976 First passenger flights on a
supersonic aeroplane: Concorde

Discussion

How many of these kinds of transport have you travelled on?
Is transport a problem where you live? If so, why?
What different forms of transport do you need to get from your home to:

a   your school or workplace?   b   your nearest cinema?   c   the nearest airport?

2 Conversation

1   Listen.

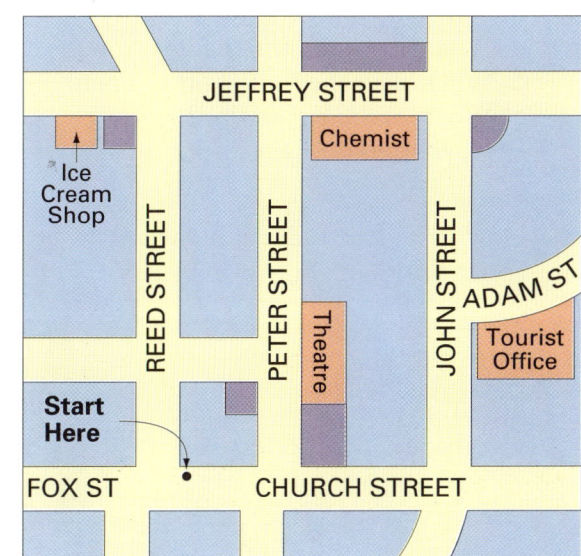

Woman: Excuse me. Could you tell me how often the number 6 bus comes?
Bus driver: You've just missed it, I'm afraid, but there's another one in half an hour.
Woman: Oh no! In that case, could you tell me where the tourist office is?
Bus driver: Certainly. Go down this street, take the second on the left and the first on the right. That's Adam Street, and the tourist office is on your right.
Woman: Thank you. And just one more thing. Do you know where Fox Street is?
Bus driver: Madam, this *is* Fox Street! Can't you see the sign over there?
Woman: Oh, yes! Thanks a lot!

2   Now listen and mark these places on the map.

a   bus station   b   taxi rank   c   bus stop   d   underground station   e   car park

3 **Pronunciation:** Question intonation

1   Direct questions usually have falling intonation:

How often does the bus come?

Where is the nearest taxi rank?

Indirect questions usually have rising intonation:

Can you tell me how often the bus comes?

Could you tell me where to catch the airport bus?

2   Now listen and practise.

Where is Adam Street?   What time does the last train go?
Could you tell me where Adam Street is?   Do you know what time the last train goes?

4 **Grammar focus:** Direct and indirect questions

Direct questions with *be*	Indirect questions with *be*
Where is the bank?	Can you tell me **where** the bank **is**?
Where is Adam Street?	Do you know **where** Adam Street **is**?
Direct questions with *do*	Indirect questions
How often does the bus **come**?	Can you tell me **how often** the bus **comes**?
When do the banks **open**?	Could you tell me **when** the banks **open**?
What time does the market **close**?	Do you know **what time** the market **closes**?

1   Make indirect questions from these direct questions.

   a   How much does a taxi to the airport cost?
   b   Where is the nearest underground station?
   c   What time does the last bus come?
   d   When does the tourist office open?
   e   Where is the bus station?
   f   How often does the airport bus leave?

2   Now write four indirect questions about things in your town or city.

3   *Pair work*

   Take turns asking your questions. Use rising intonation.

5 **Word power:** Landmarks

1 Write these places in the chart below.

bank   petrol station   multi-storey car park cinema
library   passport office hotel   bookshop
the National Gallery sports complex railway station   newsagent
stationer's

Commercial buildings	Government buildings	Transport facilities	Arts and entertainment	Shops
bank				

2 Now add the names of two places in your nearest town or city to each list.

3 *Class activity*

Which are the five most important landmarks in your town or city?

6 **Conversation**

1 Listen.

Stranger: Excuse me, please. Do you know where the nearest bank is?
Local man: Well, the City Bank isn't far from here.
     Do you know where the post office is?
Stranger: No, not really. I'm just passing through.
Local man: Well, first go down this street to
     the traffic lights.
Stranger: Yes.
Local man: Then turn left into North Street
     and the bank is on your right,
     just past the post office.
Stranger: All right. Thanks a lot.
Local man: Not at all.

2 Now listen to the rest of the conversation.
Who did the man telephone?
Why?

7 Grammar focus: Sequence markers and imperatives 🎞

> **First go** down this street to the traffic lights.
> **Next turn** right and **go** along King Street for about 500 metres.
> **Then look** for the Hilton Hotel.
> **After that go** up the little street beside it.
> **Finally cross** the bridge and you're there.

Number the sentences from 1 to 11 to make a conversation. Then practise it with a partner.

A

.... Did you say Blade Street?

.... I'm trying to find La Taverna restaurant.

.... Excuse me, I'm lost.

.... OK. Thanks very much.

.... To the traffic lights, OK.

.... In Henderson Avenue. Could you tell me how to get there, please?

B

.... Well, first go along Nathan Road to the traffic lights.

.... Oh, I know where that is. It's in Henderson Avenue.

.... No, Blake Street. Go down Blake Street until you get to Henderson Avenue. La Taverna is on the left.

.... After that cross the street and then go down Blake Street.

.... Oh, what are you looking for?

8 Here and there

Pair work

Take turns giving directions to these or other places near your class.

a post office
a newsagent
a cinema
a bank
a supermarket
a coffee shop

Useful words and phrases

across
along
up/down the street
in front of/behind
near
next to/beside
in
on the corner of
opposite
on the right/left

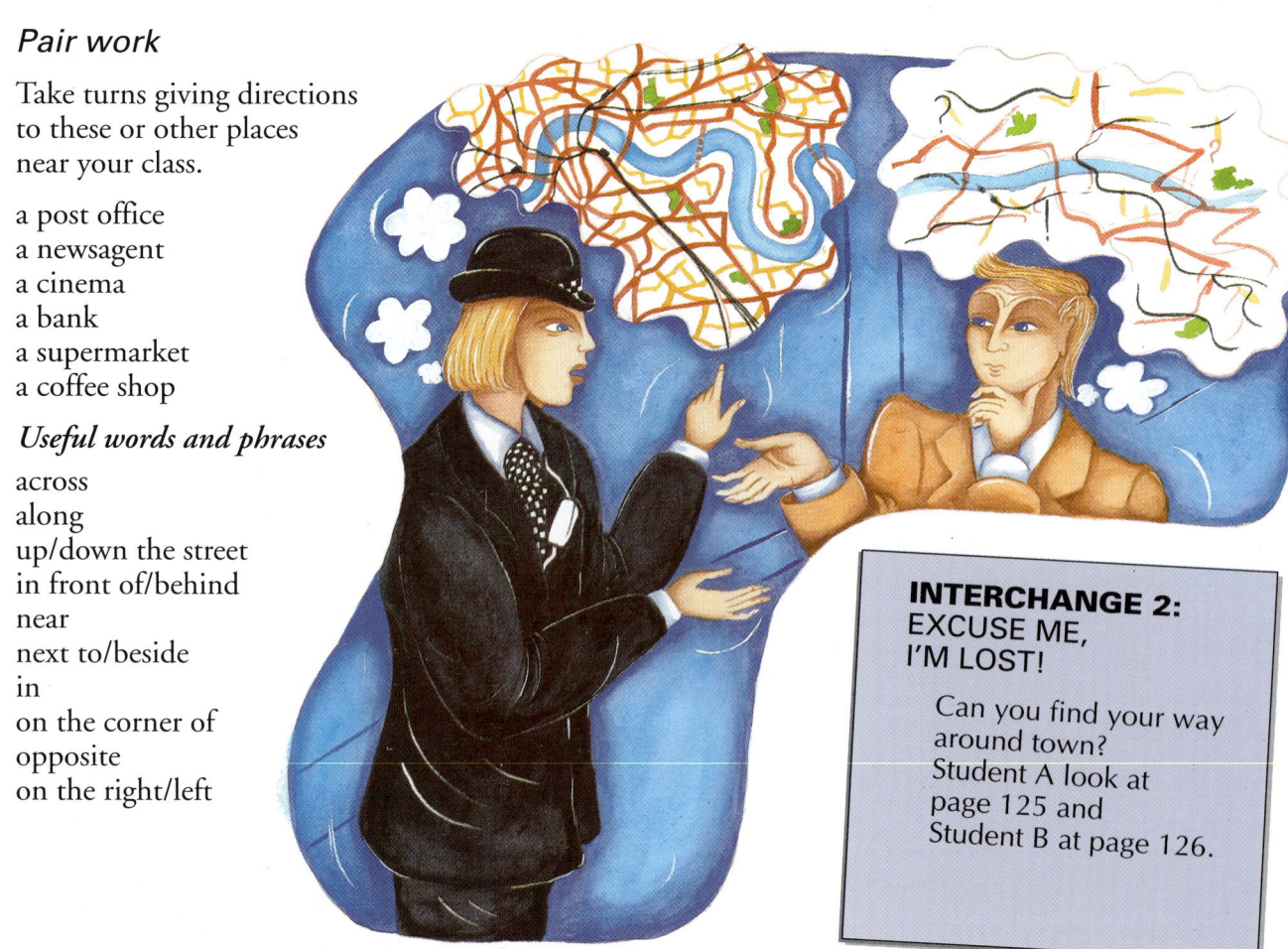

> **INTERCHANGE 2:**
> **EXCUSE ME,**
> **I'M LOST!**
>
> Can you find your way around town? Student A look at page 125 and Student B at page 126.

9 Listening 🔲

1 Martin is explaining how to get to his house. Listen and number five of the pictures from 1 to 5 in the order you hear them.

HILL STREET

....

....

....

2 Now listen to the conversation again and take notes.

3 *Pair work*

Use your notes and describe how to get to Martin's house.

10 Writing

1 Write directions to get to your home from this class.

> I live at 13 Cedar Drive. The best way to get there is by bus. First, get a number 16 bus from the Town Hall and get off at Hanley Road. Then ...

> I live in Garden City. To get there by car, take the A1 from here for about ten miles. Turn left at Hampton village into Wilson Avenue. From there ...

2 *Pair work*

Take turns reading your directions. Your partner takes notes or draws a map.

3 Now use your notes or map and check the directions to your partner's home, like this.

OK, you live at 13 Cedar Drive. First, I take a number 16 bus ...

11 Reading

Read about this walking tour of Chichester and draw the route on the map.

The Roman city of Chichester

Why not give yourself a refreshing change and have a gentle walk round the old Roman city of Chichester?

Start at the station and turn left into Southgate. Walk along into South Street past the Tourist Information office. Turn left into Canon Lane and right into St Richard's Walk where you will see the magnificent Cathedral in front of you. This beautiful building was started in 1091 and is well worth visiting. On leaving the Cathedral, walk back along West Street towards the Market Cross where the four main streets meet. Here you are in the heart of the pedestrian shopping area and can browse at leisure round the varied shops, pubs, restaurants and tea rooms.

Leave the Market Cross by North Street and take the second on your right along St Peter's to Priory Park. Here you will find the Guildhall Museum, first used by monks 600 years ago. Now it is a wonderful building to explore and has exhibitions about its history and about the park. From here – after a rest in the park – you can walk south along the top of the old city walls, leaving them to go down East Row on your right. On the corner of East Row and Little London you will find the District Museum with its displays of Roman life in the area.

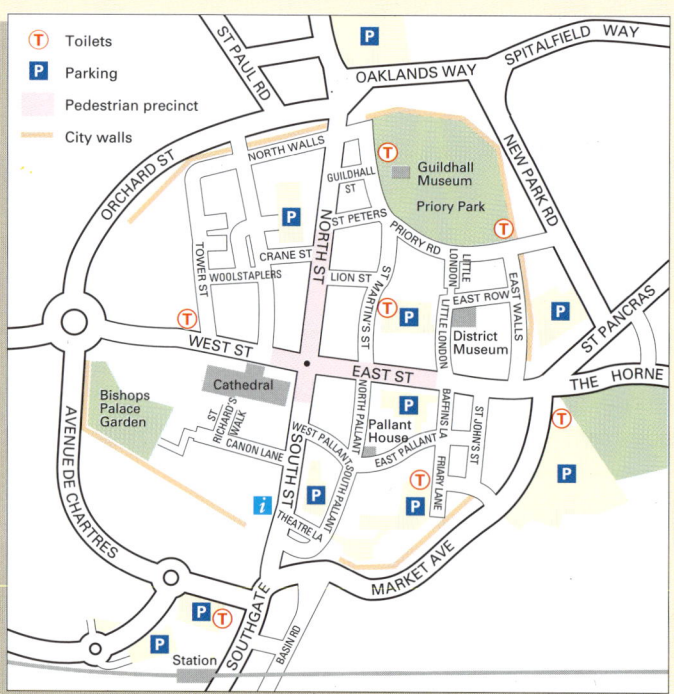

Step out of the Museum into Little London, and stop for one of the best teas in England at the Shepherd's Tea Rooms. From here you will find yourself quickly back in East Street in the pedestrian area.

If you are not too tired, have a look at Pallant House, in North Pallant, built in 1712, and now a historic house and art gallery. From here it is a short walk back to the station along South Pallant, turning right into Theatre Lane and then left into Southgate which leads you back to the train station.

Try to come to Chichester in July when there is an internationally famous festival of music, theatre, comedy, street entertainment and much, much more.

Unit summary

Grammar

Direct questions and indirect questions: singular and plural

Where **is** the **shop**?	Could you tell me where the **shop is**?
Where **are** the **shops**?	Could you tell me where the **shops are**?
How often **does** the bus **come**?	Can you tell me how often the **bus comes**?
How often **do** the **buses** come?	Can you tell me how often the **buses come**?

For the past tense of irregular verbs, see page 142.

Key vocabulary

Nouns
airport
arts
bank
bookshop
bridge
building
bus
bus station
bus stop
car park
cinema
coffee shop
department store
garage
gift shop
hotel
library
market
National Gallery
newsagent
passport office
post office
science museum
shopping centre
sports complex
stationer's
street
supermarket
taxi rank
town hall
traffic lights
transport
underground entrance
underground station

Verbs
catch
close
cost
cross
find
know
leave
look for
miss
open

say
tell
try
turn

Modal verbs
can
could

Adjectives
commercial
good
last
little
lost
nearest

Adverbs
about
after that
around here
down
finally
first
left
next
past
right
then

Prepositions
across
along
behind
beside
down
in front of
in the middle of
near
next to
on the corner of
on your left
on your right
opposite
up

Directions
east
north
south
west

Other words
another one
one
some
there's

Time expressions
an hour
a quarter of an hour
half an hour
three quarters of an hour
forty-five minutes

Expressions
Excuse me.
Oh, no!
Just one more thing.
Certainly.
Oh!
Thanks a lot.
Not at all.
Well …
Not really.
OK.
All right.
Let me tell you how to get there.
In that case …

A home of your own

Describing and comparing homes, neighbourhoods and towns

comparatives
... *not as* ...

1 Word power: Houses

1 Where would you find these things in a house or a flat? Write the names in the floor plan, in the room where you would find them. Then compare with a partner.

basin	oven
carpet	shower
chest of drawers	sink
coffee table	sofa
freezer	washing machine
lamp	wardrobe

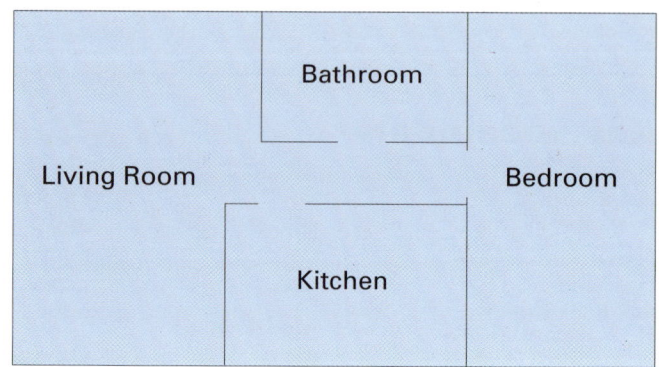

Bathroom

Living Room

Bedroom

Kitchen

2 Now add as many words as you can to the floor plan. Write them in the room where they belong.

2 Conversation

1 Listen.

Mr Andrews: Hello?

Mr Jones: Hello, Mr Andrews? This is Max Jones from Ripley's Estate Agent's.

Mr Andrews: Oh, hello, Mr Jones! Have you found a house for me yet?

Mr Jones: Yes, I've got a wonderful house to show you in Padley Drive. It's only £120 000.

Mr Andrews: Oh, I'm sorry, but that's much too expensive for me!

Mr Jones: Not to worry! I've got another one in Bank Street. It's only £45 000, but it's only got one bedroom.

Mr Andrews: Not big enough, I'm afraid.

Mr Jones: Well, how about a house in the country? About 100 miles from London, near Southampton.

Mr Andrews: That sounds interesting. Tell me more!

Mr Jones: Well, it's fairly old, so it needs a little work. But it's within your price range at £80 000 and I'm sure you'll like it. It's really beautiful.

2 Listen to the end of the conversation. What else does the estate agent say about the house?

3 Grammar focus: Adjectives and adverbs 📼

> What's your house like?
>
> It's **too** small.   It's **awfully** small.
> It's **not very** big.   **really**
> It's **not** big **enough**.   **very**
> It's big **enough**.   **quite**
>   **fairly**

1   Write sentences that have similar meanings to the sentences below. Use the grammar box above and the words in the list below.

My flat is too small. or It's not big enough.

a This area is not clean enough.   expensive
b The town centre is not very safe at night.   dirty
c My flat is quite cheap.   cool
d It's too warm here in the summer.   interesting
e This town is really boring.   dangerous

2   Now match these questions with suitable responses. More than one response may be possible.

a What's the weather like?
b Do you live in a nice part of town?
c What's your house/flat like?
d What's your town like to live in?

.... It's fairly small, but it's in a good area.

.... It's very cold in the winter, but it's quite nice in the summer.

.... It's very crowded and it's awfully polluted.

.... It's really comfortable and the rent is reasonable, too.

.... It's expensive to live here, but it's a really exciting place.

.... It's all right, but it's too far from the centre of town.

.... It's quite nice, and the people are very friendly.

3   Write six sentences about your home, neighbourhood or town. Then compare with a partner.

4 What's it like?

Pair work

Take turns asking about one of these places.

Your favourite city

What is your favourite city?
What's it like?
Is it expensive to live there?
What's the transport like?
What's the weather like?
Is it ...?

Your house or flat

Do you live in a house or a flat?
What's it like?
Is it ...?
How ... is it?
What's the area like?
What are your neighbours like?

5 Listening 🎙

1 Listen to people phoning about
three of these advertisements and
number them 1 to 3 in the order
you hear them.

....

....

....

Camden Town Top
floor studio £400
p.c.m. Phone Mr
Marsh 071 893 5340

Parkwood Gardens
1 bdrm flt £300 071
894 4621 eves

Large sunny room in
quiet house in Elm
Ave. Share facilities.
£180 inc.

2 bedroom house
near hospital. £450.
081 563 7613

Spring Street 2
bedroom flat with
view. Partly furnished.
£350 exc. 081 341
2435

In Newton Square 3
bed 2 bath house
w/garden. £600. 071
672 1246

....

....

....

2 Now listen again and take notes. What other information do you hear about each place?

6 Snapshot

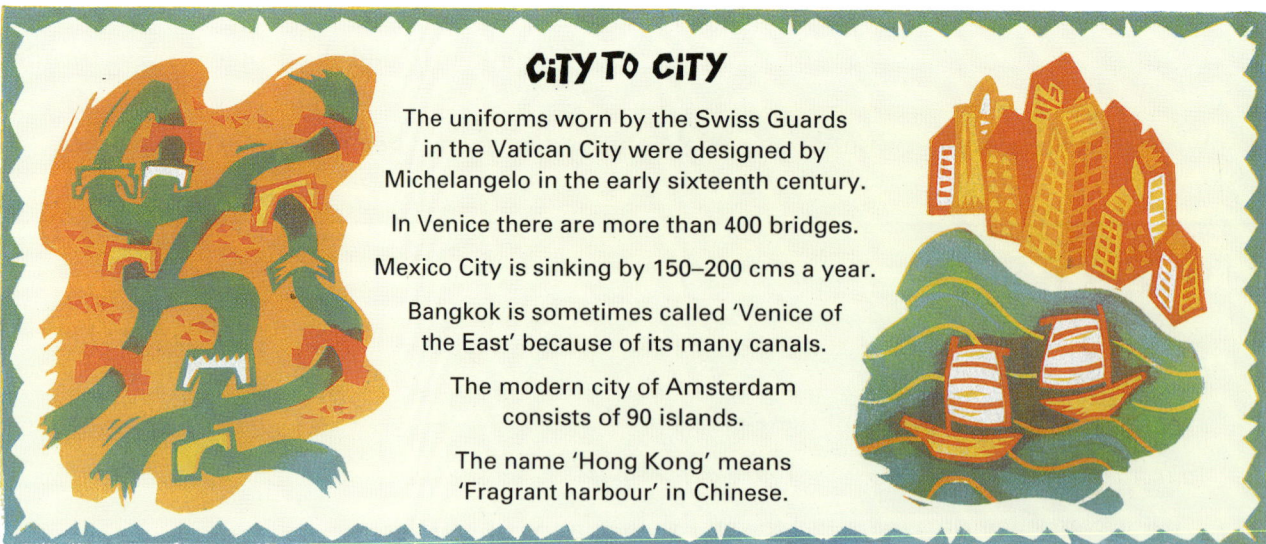

CITY TO CITY

The uniforms worn by the Swiss Guards
in the Vatican City were designed by
Michelangelo in the early sixteenth century.

In Venice there are more than 400 bridges.

Mexico City is sinking by 150–200 cms a year.

Bangkok is sometimes called 'Venice of
the East' because of its many canals.

The modern city of Amsterdam
consists of 90 islands.

The name 'Hong Kong' means
'Fragrant harbour' in Chinese.

Discussion

Do you know anything else about the cities above?
Tell the class two unusual facts about any cities you know.

7 Conversation

1 Listen.

Jack: Someone told me hotels are really expensive in Amsterdam.
Terry: Yes, but not as expensive as Paris. You can pay £200 a night there.
Jack: As much as that?
Terry: Yes, it's very expensive.
Jack: But which do you think is more interesting?
Terry: Well, Paris is good for sightseeing, but Amsterdam is much more exciting, especially at night!

2 Listen to the rest of the conversation.
What does Terry say about the nightlife in Amsterdam?

8 Grammar focus: Comparison of adjectives

With adjective + *er*	with *more/less* + adjective
Paris is **bigger than** Amsterdam.	Paris is **more crowded than** Amsterdam.
Amsterdam is (**much**) **smaller**.	Amsterdam is (**much**) **less crowded**.
Amsterdam is **not as big as** Paris.	Paris is **not as relaxed as** Amsterdam.
It's **not as old**.	It's **not as cheap**.

See page 143 for comparative forms.

1 Use two words to complete these sentences.

a London is more .... Lisbon. (expensive)
b Public transport in Paris is .... in London. (cheap)
c Sardinia is much less .... Hong Kong. (crowded)
d Rio de Janeiro is much .... Florence. (large)
e The weather in Edinburgh is not as .... in Rome. (nice)
f Oslo is much .... in winter .... Tangiers. (cold)
g London is not as .... in summer .... Madrid. (hot)

2 Now write six sentences like these about cities you know and read them to a partner.

9 Pronunciation: Sentence stress

1 We stress words that carry the most important information.

Paris is **bigger** than **Amsterdam**. **Amsterdam** is **not** as **big** as **Paris**.

2 Now listen and practise the sentences you completed in Exercise 8.1.

10 What's the difference?

1 Pair work

Choose two big towns in your country and two other big towns you know. How are they different? Discuss some of these topics.

size	people
weather	entertainment
transport	shopping
cost of living	food
housing	problems

A: Let's compare Paris and …
B: All right. And let's talk about food first.
A: OK. I think the food in Paris is …
B: Yes, and …

2 Class activity

Tell the class which cities you compared and some of the differences you found.

11 Writing

1

Write about two of the cities you compared in Exercise 10 or two other places you know about.

There are many differences between Frankfurt and Athens. Athens is much older than Frankfurt and Frankfurt has more modern buildings. Athens is cheaper …

2 Pair work

Swap papers. Ask your partner questions about the places in her/his composition.

12 Listening 🔲

Listen and choose the correct response.

a .... Yes, Rome is better.
  .... Yes, it is.
b .... Brazil is bigger.
  .... No, it's not as big.
c .... Yes, much warmer.
  .... Yes, much smaller.

d .... Yes, much hotter.
  .... Yes, it's more expensive.
e .... Yes, much more difficult.
  .... No, it's not as old.
f .... Yes, it's not as good.
  .... Yes, it's much better.

13 **Reading:** Town or country?

1   Read this information from an estate agent about two kinds of property for sale.

Princess Elisabeth House

General description
A beautifully presented ground floor flat forming part of a Regency property of architectural and historical interest. On the south coast, 50 miles from London, this house is divided into six flats and has a communal entrance fitted with a video entry phone. The flat has a kitchen, 2 reception rooms, 2 bedrooms and a bathroom.

Situation
The property is situated on the sea front and only a short walking distance from the shopping streets of St George's Road and St James's Street. An excellent bus service runs every 6 mins to the town centre and the railway station, with trains to London every 15 minutes. Parking is possible with a resident's permit — currently £100 a year.

Manor House

General description
Manor House is a beautiful period house, set in 5 acres of land, with two garages and a spacious barn. It has 4 bedrooms, a luxury bathroom, a large reception room, a kitchen and utility room. It is centrally heated throughout. It needs some decoration.

Situation
15 miles from Ridgewell, a busy town with all facilities, and 35 miles from London, Manor House is surrounded by rolling countryside and farmland. It is served by a station at Hunton Bridge, 6 miles away, where hourly trains run to London. It has some local shops and is close to both primary and secondary schools.

2   Find five differences between the properties.

Which property do you think is best for …
a a family with young children, husband working at home?
b a young couple without a car, buying their first property?
c a retired couple whose family often come to visit them?

3   Which property would you prefer to live in? Why?

> **INTERCHANGE 3:**
> HOUSING SURVEY
>
> Where do other people in your class live? Find out about their homes with the survey on page 127.

Unit summary

Grammar

Comparisons: Questions with *which* ...?

> Which is **more interesting**, Amsterdam or Paris?
> Which is **bigger**, Hamburg or Frankfurt?

Irregular adjectives

> The weather is **good**.
>   **not as good as** in Hawaii.
>   **better than** in Hawaii.
> The transport is **bad**.
>   **not as bad as** in London.
>   **worse than** in London.

For a list of comparative forms of adjectives, see page 143.

Key vocabulary

Nouns
air conditioning
alarm clock
area
basin
bathroom
bedroom
carpet
central heating
centre
chest of drawers
coffee table
cost of living
country
dishwasher
entertainment
estate agent
flat
food
freezer
hotel
house
housing
lamp
living room
microwave
neighbour
neighbourhood
nightlife
oven
people
place
price range
problem
rent
shopping
shower
sightseeing

sink
size
sofa
summer
town
transport
wardrobe
washing machine
weather
winter

Verbs
need
pay
show

Adjectives
all right
beautiful
big
boring
cheap
clean
cold
comfortable
cool
crowded
dangerous
difficult
dirty
exciting
expensive
friendly
furnished
hot
interesting
large
lovely
modern

nice
noisy
old
polluted
pretty
quiet
reasonable
relaxed
safe
small
ugly
warm
wonderful

Adverbs
at night
awfully
especially
fairly
more
much more
only
quite
really
too
very
yet

Conjunctions
so

Other words
enough
less ... than
more ... than
(not) as ... as

Expressions
How about ...?
That sounds interesting.
Let's compare ... and ...
Let's talk about ...
What's ... like?
It needs a little work.

1-3 Review

1 Conversation

Pair work

Take turns talking about yourself.

A: So, can I ask you a few questions about yourself?
B: …
A: Where did you live as a child?
B: …
A: I see. And did you go to school there?
B: …
A: Really? And what games did you use to like to play as a child?
B: …
A: Oh? Who was your best friend when you were younger?
B: …
A: What was she/he like?
B: …
A: And what did you and she/he use to do together?
B: …

2 How times have changed!

1 *Group work*

Take turns talking about how family life has changed since your grandparents' young days. Ask questions like these.

Were families usually bigger or smaller in your grandparents' time?
What kinds of houses did people live in then?
Do you think people in your grandparents' time worked more than they do today?
What kinds of jobs did men use to have?
What about women?
How were schools different?
How is housework different today? Is it easier or more difficult?
What machines have you got in your house that your grandparents didn't use to have?
In what other ways do you think life was different in your grandparents' time?

2 *Class activity*

Compare answers. Do you think life was better then? Why? Why not?

3 Listening 📼

Listen to people asking for information, and choose the correct response.

a ... It's just around the corner.
   ... Yes, it closes at 3.00.
b ... Yes, it does.
   ... The next one is in ten minutes.
c ... On the corner of High Street and Walker Street.
   ... At nine o'clock in the morning.

d ... Yes, it is.
   ... It's very crowded.
e ... No, I don't.
   ... It's very exciting.
f ... By bus.
   ... I'm sorry. I'm a stranger here.

---

4 Where am I going?

1 Pair work

Think of a well-known building or place (e.g., a bank, restaurant, office building, shop) within walking distance of your class. Write down the easiest way to get there from class.

> *First, go outside and turn left. Walk straight down the road to the traffic lights. Turn right into ...*

End your directions like this (but don't give the name of the place).

> *It's a large grey building on the corner of River Road and Main Avenue. You can't miss it!*

2 Class activity

Read your directions to the class. Other students try to guess the name of the building or place.

---

5 Differences

1 Choose one of these pairs and compare them. How many differences can you think of?

a restaurant and a fast food restaurant
a market and a department store

Talk about them like this.

People are more friendly in a ...
You don't use a credit card in a ...
Prices are cheaper in a ...
It's more expensive in a ...

2 Class activity

Compare the differences.

I've never heard of it!

Talking about food and ways of preparing food
Past simple
Present perfect
Two-part verbs *with, up, in, out, on, off, over*

1 Snapshot

ETHNIC FAVOURITES

China
Beggar's chicken:

Chicken, mushrooms
and vegetables,
wrapped in paper and
clay, and baked

Great Britain
Devonshire scones:

Small baked buns made
of flour, butter and milk,
served with whipped
cream and jam

Indonesia
Gado Gado:

A salad made with
sliced vegetables,
eggs and a thick
peanut sauce

Greece
Moussaka:

A baked dish with
minced lamb, tomatoes,
aubergines, cheese
and a white sauce

Complete the information below. Then compare with a partner.

My favourite food: .... Food I really don't like: ....

The most unusual food I've ever eaten: ....

Discussion

How often do you eat out? What do you usually order?

2 Conversation

1 Listen.

Helen: Hey, this sounds good – snails with
garlic. Have you ever eaten snails?
Tony: No, I haven't, actually.
Helen: Oh, they're delicious! I had them
last time. Like to try some?
Tony: No, thanks. They sound strange.
Waitress: Have you decided on a starter, yet?
Helen: Yes, I'll have the snails, please.
Waitress: And you, sir?
Tony: I think I'll have the fried brains.
Helen: Now *that* sounds strange!

2 Now listen to the rest of the conversation.
Did Tony like the fried brains? What else did he order?

3 Grammar focus: Past simple and present perfect 🔲

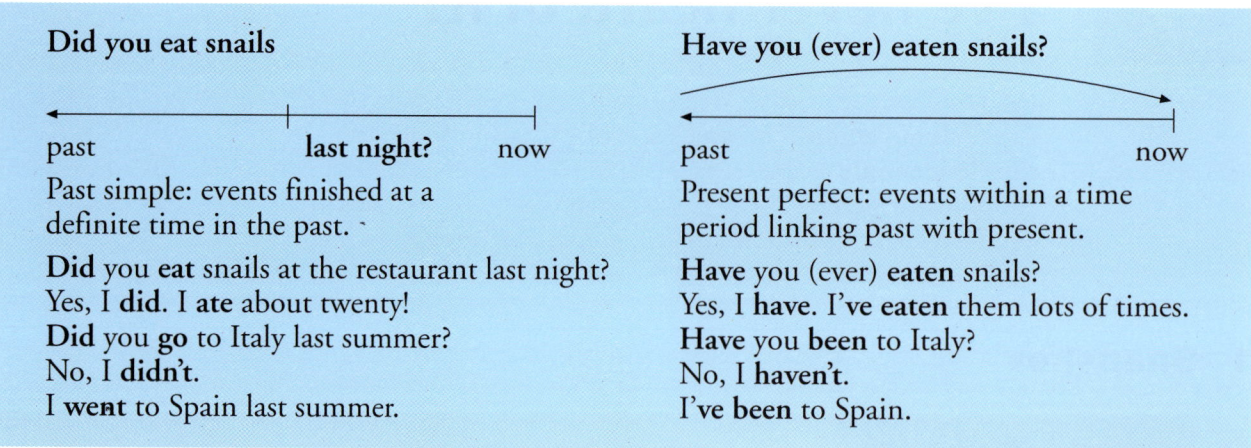

Did you eat snails	**Have you (ever) eaten snails?**
←————————————|————————————→	←——————————————————————→
past **last night?** now	past now
Past simple: events finished at a definite time in the past.	Present perfect: events within a time period linking past with present.
Did you **eat** snails at the restaurant last night? Yes, I **did**. I **ate** about twenty!	**Have** you (ever) **eaten** snails? Yes, I **have**. I've **eaten** them lots of times.
Did you **go** to Italy last summer? No, I **didn't**.	**Have** you **been** to Italy? No, I **haven't**.
I **went** to Spain last summer.	I've **been** to Spain.

Complete these conversations and then practise them with a partner. (See page 142 for verb forms.)

a A: Have you ever .... (be) on a rollercoaster?

   B: Yes, I .... It was fun!

b A: Did you .... (go) to the cinema last weekend?

   B: No, I .... I was too busy.

c A: Did you .... (have) a holiday last year?

   B: Yes, I .... I went skiing.

d A: Have you .... (have) a holiday this year?

   B: No, I .... Not yet.

---

4 Find out more!

Pair work

Ask your partner these questions and four more of your own.

Did you …
learn how to type at school?
eat out last weekend?
do anything interesting last night?
drive to class today?

Have you ever …
eaten frogs' legs?
flown in a helicopter?
been skiing?
been to a fortune teller?

---

5 Listening 🔲

Listen to this conversation between a dietician and a patient. Complete the dietician's notes.

Patient's name *Robert Merridrew*	Age	Weight ....
Profession	Smoker now?	In the past? ....
Brief description of any illness or symptoms		
Diet	Exercise	
Recommendations		

6 Word power

1 Write these words in the chart below. Then add two more words to each column.

cabbage   crisps   mineral water   peanuts   tablespoon
cheesecake   ice cream   onion   saucepan   tomato juice

Drinks	Snacks	Vegetables	Desserts	Utensils
....	....	....	....	....
....	....	....	....	....
....	....	....	....	....
....	....	....	....	....

2 *Pair work*

Now use six of these words in questions to ask your partner.

Have you ever tried chocolate cheesecake?

7 Pronunciation: Word stress 🔲

1 Are these words stressed
on the 1st or 2nd syllable?

banana   coffee   dessert   pizza   restaurant
chicken   delicious   orange   potato   vegetable

Now listen and check.

2 Listen and underline the stressed syllable in the words in Exercise 6.
Take turns reading the words aloud with a partner. Check the correct stress.

8 Conversation 🔲

1 Listen.

Helga: What's that you're making?
Richard: My favourite! A club sandwich!
Helga: I've never heard of it! How do you make it?
Richard: It's easy, but it depends on what's in the
          fridge. You cut up some lettuce, tomato,
          prawns and hard boiled eggs and make
          a large sandwich with toasted bread.
Helga: We haven't got any prawns.
Richard: Chicken or tuna fish is fine.
Helga: Shall I put some mayonnaise in?
Richard: Yes, if you like. That looks great!
          Thanks a lot!
Helga: Hey! Wait a minute! Where's mine?

2 *Pair work*

Cover the conversation. Can you remember how to make a club sandwich?

9 Grammar focus: Two-part verbs 🔲

With nouns		With pronouns
Cut up the lettuce.	**Cut** the lettuce **up.**	**Cut** it **up.** (Not: Cut up it.)
Put in the sugar.	**Put** the sugar **in.**	**Put** it **in.** (Not: Put in it.)

1   Put the words in brackets in appropriate places in these sentences.
Then compare with a partner.

a Pick some fresh fish and vegetables from the market and then put them the
  refrigerator until you are ready to cook. (up, in)
b Get your cookbook and look the recipe. (out, up)
c Turn the oven and set it at 300 degrees. (on)
d Cut the vegetables and put them a pan. (up, in)
e Put the fish a dish and pour the sauce it. (in, over)
f Make sure you wash the dishes when you have finished. (up)
g Put the dry dishes the cupboard. (in)

2   *Pair work*

Complete this recipe with the two-part verbs below.
Some of them can be used more than once.

chop up	pour on	put on	take out
cut up	put in	take off	turn over

Barbecued kebabs

a First, ... some wood
  and .... it .... the barbecue,
  or use some charcoal.

b Then .... some lighter fluid ....
  and light the fire.

c Now .... the meat and
  vegetables, and .... them .... a
  small bowl with some sauce.

d .... them .... of the bowl after
  twenty minutes.

e Then .... the meat and vegetables
  .... the skewers and .... them
  .... the barbecue.

f .... the kebabs .... after ten minutes
  and cook them for 10–15 minutes more.

g Then .... the kebabs .... the
  barbecue and eat!

10 Listening 📼

Listen to these people describing how to make the things below. One ingredient in each description is wrong. What is it?

a banana milkshake   b omelette   c vegetable salad   d iced lemon tea

11 Snacks in a second

1   Make notes about your favourite quick snack.

What is it called? What ingredients do you need to make it? How do you make it?

2   *Pair work*

Take turns describing how to make your favourite quick snack.

A: What's your favourite snack?
B: It's ...
A: What do you need to make it?
B: You need ...
A: How do you make it?
B: First, you ... After that, ... Next, ... Then ...

3   *Class activity*

Which students had interesting snacks? Tell the class how to make them.

12 Writing: Recipes

1   Write the recipe for one of your favourite meals. First write a list of ingredients. Then use some of the words below to say how it is prepared.

fried	served with	fresh
boiled	filled with	dried
grilled	mixed with	spicy
baked	cooked with	hot

Now write your recipe.

> This recipe is for chicken curry. You need chicken, onions
> First you cut up the chicken, and then fry the small pieces
> lightly in oil

INTERCHANGE 4:
THE SECRET
PASTS!

Find out more about other students' secret pasts!
Turn to page 126.

2   *Group work*

Swap the recipes and read them.
Make a note of any you would like to try.

13 Reading: Would you like to go out for a meal?

1 Read these statements. Then read the reviews. Are the statements true (**T**) or false (**F**)?

You have to book at all these restaurants.
You have to pay a service charge at all these restaurants.
Only one restaurant doesn't have music.
One restaurant offers free drinks.

1

The New Tapas House

Never know what to choose when you go out to eat? Try The New Tapas House and choose them all! A selection of 3 or 4 small dishes offers you the best in fish, meat and vegetarian delicacies in special Spanish style. We ordered grilled sardines (£3.50), deep fried potatoes in spicy sauce (£2.20), meatballs in tomato sauce (£3.50), artichoke in vinaigrette (£3.00), garlic bread (£1.30) and a mixed salad (£3.50). All were deliciously prepared and we

washed them down with freshly squeezed orange juice – free on every table. Background live Spanish guitar music made the evening more authentic and enjoyable. Service included. Booking essential on 691023.

2

La Piazza

This lively but loud Italian restaurant offers fast, cheerful service and a good variety of pasta and pizza dishes, as well as other main dishes, if you can take the noise! Taped Italian arias played non-stop while we were there, and this made relaxing difficult, but the food kept our attention. I had Vitello Cordon Bleu (grilled veal stuffed with cheese and mushrooms in a white sauce) £9.95 and my friend had Pollo al Mango (breast of chicken with mango and mozzarella cheese) £7.50. For dessert, the mouthwatering selection of Banoffi Pie,

Tiramisu, profiteroles and ice cream ensured that we weren't hungry when we left the restaurant. Service is included and there is no need to book at this 4-storey restaurant – you never have to wait for more than a few minutes.

3

The Royal Tandoori

This quiet, often almost deserted restaurant is a great find if you want a quiet spot to take your partner for that special occasion. The menu is endless with 25 appetisers to choose from, from Dahl soup to King Prawn Butterfly and many more main dishes from the very mild Kurmas to the very hot Pall dishes – not recommended for beginners! Main courses average £5.00, and Starters about £2.50. As you will probably want water with your meal, the total cost of your evening's eating can be very low – but remember service is not included. Booking is not usually necessary but you can ring 548921 to check.

2 **Pair work**

Find words in the passages which mean:

without meat (1)   to reserve a table (2)   empty (3)   realistic (1)
made sure (2)   not strong (3)   necessary (1)

3 Which of these restaurants would you prefer to go to?

Unit summary

Grammar

1   Countable and uncountable nouns

Countable singular	Countable plural	Uncountable
a bean	(some) beans	butter
a dish	(some) dishes	cheese
an egg	(some) eggs	chicken
a meal	(some) meals	cream
a mushroom	(some) mushrooms	flour
a recipe	(some) recipes	garlic
a sandwich	(some) sandwiches	honey
a snack	(some) snacks	jam
a spice	(some) spices	juice
a tomato	(some) tomatoes	lamb
a vegetable	(some) vegetables	milk
		meat
		oil
		paper
		tea

Words often used with uncountable nouns:

a bag of sugar	**a pound/kilo of** butter
a bottle of wine	**a piece of** cake
a bowl of soup	**a slice of** bread
a can of lemonade	**a packet of** biscuits
a carton of milk	**a tablespoon of** sugar
a jar of jam	**a teaspoon of** salt

2   For past tense of irregular verbs, see page 142.

Key vocabulary

Nouns
aubergine
banana
barbecue
bowl
butter
brains
bread
cabbage
cheese
cheesecake
chicken
class
cream
crisps
dessert
egg
fish
food
fortune teller
frog
garlic
helicopter
homework
ice cream
ingredient
jam

kebab
leg
lemon
lettuce
lighter fluid
mayonnaise
milkshake
mineral water
mushroom
oil
omelette
onion
orange
peanut
piece
pizza
prawn
recipe
rollercoaster
sandwich
sauce
saucepan
sir
snack
snail
spinach
starter

sugar
tablespoon
tomato
tuna fish
utensil
vegetable
weekend

Verbs
decide
drive
eat
eat out
fly
go skiing
learn how to
make
put
sound
try
type

Two-part verbs
chop up
cut up
get out
look up
pick up

pour on
pour over
put in
put on
take off
take out
turn on
turn over
wash up

Adjectives
baked
boiled
busy
delicious
dried
favourite
fried
grilled
hot
spicy
strange
toasted

Adverbs
ever
last
last year

this year
yesterday

Other words
anything
please

Days of the week
Monday
Tuesday
Wednesday
Thursday
Friday
Saturday
Sunday

Expressions
I've never heard of it!
Like to try some?
I think I'll …
It depends on …

Going places

Talking about plans	*going to*
Modals of advice and necessity	*must/have to*
Present continuous	*don't have to*

1 Snapshot

TRAVEL FACTS

The five top holiday destinations in Europe: Italy, Spain, France, Austria, UK

The biggest spenders on tourism: The Germans

The most visited city: Paris

The most frequently taken item from the Plaza Hotel, New York: Bathrobes (200 a month)

Discussion

What are the most popular places in your country for tourists?
What are the three places in the world you would most like to visit?

2 Word power: Travel

1   *Pair work*

Add these words to the word map.

credit card
health insurance
medicines
money belt
passport
penknife
plane tickets
rucksack
shorts
sleeping bag
swimwear
tent
traveller's cheques
vaccination
visa

Clothing
....
....
....
....

Camping gear
....
....
....
....

Money
....
....
....
....

Camping trip

Travel documents
....
....
....

Health
....
....
....
....

2   Now add five more words to the map.
Then compare with other students.

3 Conferences

1 Listen.

Sandra: Listen, Mum! I'm thinking
of hitchhiking around
Europe this summer.
What do you think?

Mother: Hitchhiking? I think that
sounds very dangerous!
You shouldn't go by yourself.
You ought to go with a friend.

Sandra: Yes, I've thought of that.

Mother: And you'd better talk to your
father first.

Sandra: I already have. He thinks
it's a great idea. He wants to
come with me!

2 **Class activity**

Have you ever hitchhiked?
Would you like to? Where would you like to go?

4 Grammar focus: Modals for necessity and suggestions

Describing necessity	Giving suggestions
You **must** take warm clothes.	You**'d better** talk to your father.
You **have to** get a passport.	You **ought to** go with a friend.
You **don't have to** get a visa.	You **should** take a sleeping bag.
You **need to** book a ticket.	You **shouldn't** go by yourself.

1 Give advice for someone who is thinking of taking
a holiday abroad. Then compare with a partner.

You must get a passport.
You shouldn't pack too many clothes.

a ... get a passport.
b ... pack too many clothes.
c ... book your ticket.
d ... make hotel reservations.
e ... get health insurance.
f ... check the weather.
g ... carry lots of cash.
h ... get traveller's cheques.
i ... take a lot of luggage.
j ... find out about visas.
k ... carry your wallet in a back pocket.

2 **Pair work**

Give four more pieces of advice to your partner.

5 Listening 🔲

Mike is planning to visit London. He is asking a Londoner for advice. Listen and fill in the chart.

Best time of year ....
Things to see and do ....

....

....

Things to avoid ....

6 Tips for tourists

1 *Group work*

What advice would you give tourists visiting your country?

What time of year should they visit?
What kind of clothing do you think they ought to bring?
Where should they stay?
What places should they visit?
What should they see?
Is there anything they shouldn't do?
What other advice would you give them?

2 *Class activity*

Compare your suggestions.

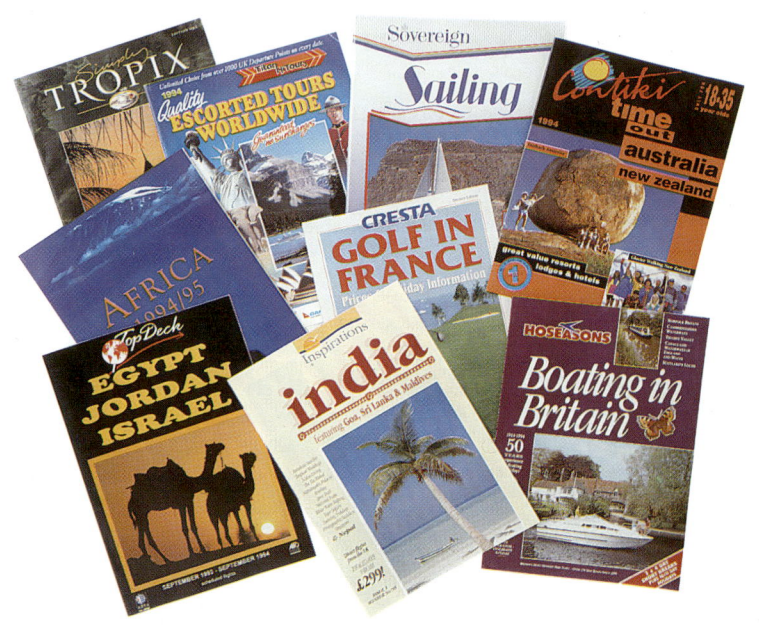

7 Conversation 🔲

1 Listen.

Pierre: What are you going to do for the long weekend, Jim?
Jim: I'm going to Scotland. Edinburgh, actually.
Pierre: What? Just for the weekend?
Jim: Why not? I'm going to take the ferry across to Dover, and then get the night bus. It should be great, just wandering around the city for a couple of days.
Pierre: Yes, it does sound a good idea. Listen, can I come too? I was planning to stay at home and do nothing, but I must say Edinburgh would be a lot more interesting.

2 Now listen to the rest of the conversation. Who does Jim know in Edinburgh, and where can they stay?

8 Pronunciation: Weak form of *going to* ▱

1 Listen to the weak form of *going to* before a verb.

What are you going to do after this class?   We're going to see a film.
    /ɡənə/   /ɡənə/

2 Listen to these sentences with the weak form of *going to*. Then practise.

What are you going to do tonight?
Are you going to go to the match on Saturday?
Where are you going to have dinner tonight?

9 Grammar focus: Present continuous and *going to* for future ▱

With present continuous	With *going to* + verb
What **are** you **doing** after class?	What **are** you **going to** do this weekend?
I'm not **doing** much.	I'm not **going to** study.
Are you **doing** anything tonight?	**Are** you **going to** do anything tonight?
Yes, I'm **meeting** a friend.	Yes, I'm **going to** see a film.

1 Complete these conversations with the present continuous or *going to*.

a A: .... you .... (do)
     anything after class?
  B: Yes, I .... (do) some shopping.
     Would you like to come?

b A: What .... you .... (do)
     tomorrow night?
  B: Nothing much. Why?
  A: Well, some of us .... (take)
     the teacher out for coffee.
     Would you like to join us?

c A: What .... you .... (do)
     on Saturday?
  B: Well, I .... (work) until four o'clock.
     Then I .... (go) to a party.
     What about you?
  A: I .... (go) away for the weekend.

2 *Pair work*

Practise the conversations above with a partner. Use the weak form of *going to* + verb.

3 Now have conversations about these times:

tonight, on Saturday night, on Sunday

10   Listening

1   Dan is going to take a trip to Central and South America. Listen to his travel plans and number the countries he is going to visit from 1–6 in the order you hear them.

NICARAGUA
COSTA RICA
COLOMBIA
ECUADOR
VENEZUELA
BRAZIL
CHILE
ARGENTINA

.... Argentina   .... Costa Rica

.... Brazil   .... Ecuador

.... Chile   .... Nicaragua

.... Colombia   .... Venezuela

2   Listen again. Who is he going with?
How long is he going to stay?

11   Dream holiday

1   *Pair work*

You've won a lot of money in a competition. Plan an interesting trip around the world with your partner. Discuss these questions and others of your own. Make notes.

Where are we going to start from?
What time of year should we travel?
How many countries and cities are we going to visit?
How long should we go for?
Which places are we going to stay in for some time?
What are we planning to do and see in these places?
How much money should we take?
What things do we need to take?

2   *Group work*

Compare your plans.
Which trip sounds the most interesting?

12   Writing: Itineraries

1   Write about the trip you planned in Exercise 11 or a real trip you plan to make.

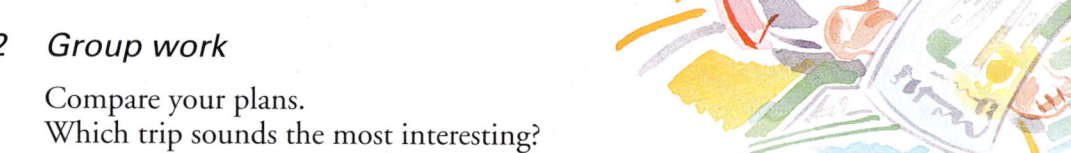

Next summer I'm going to travel round Europe on a motorbike. I'm going with two friends …

2   *Class activity*

Put your compositions on the board. Which trip would you like to make?

INTERCHANGE 5:
COASTAL FLING

Plan an interesting holiday on the coast of America. Student A look at page 128 and Student B at page 130.

13 **Reading:** Fitness in the air

1   Many people get jet lag when they travel. Here are some exercises you can do in your seat
on a long plane flight that will reduce jet lag. Match each exercise with the correct picture.

   a   Turn your head to the right and touch your shoulder with your chin.
       Then repeat to the left.
   b   Bend your back slightly, then drop your head back so that you can see the overhead
       compartment. Relax your jaw. Feel the stretch in your neck and chin.
   c   Sit up straight and lift your left foot off the floor, raising your whole leg
       about an inch off the seat. Turn your foot to the left and then
       to the right ten times. Repeat with the right foot.
   d   Sit up straight with your shoulders slightly forward.
       Put your fingers together and raise your arms to chest
       level, keeping your elbows straight and your palms
       facing outward. Stretch and then relax.
   e   Sit up straight. Hold the left armrest with your
       right hand and turn your body and head to the
       left. Release and then hold the right armrest
       with your left hand and turn to the right.

1 ....

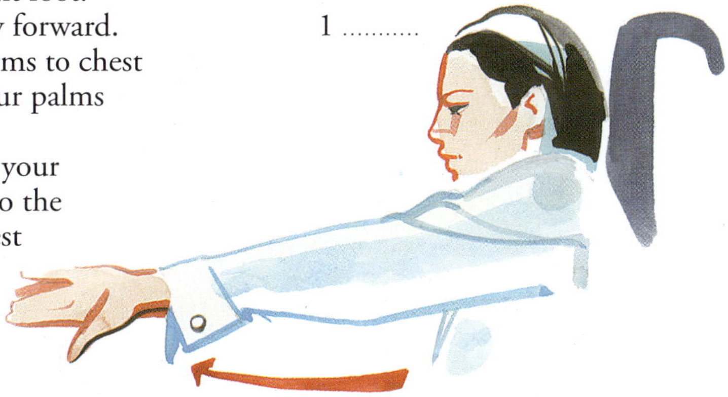

2 ....

3 ....

4 ....

5 ....

2 *Pair work*

   Take turns. Read an exercise aloud to your partner. She/He will follow your instructions.

Unit summary

Grammar

1 Modal verbs

> **Ability**
> I **can** speak Spanish.
>
> **Possibility**
> You **can** get traveller's cheques at the bank.
> You **could** go with a friend.
> You **may** need a visa.
> You **might** need a vaccination.
>
> **Suggestion**
> You **should** take traveller's cheques.
> You **shouldn't** …
> You **ought to** …
> You **could** …
> You'd **better** …
> I **would** …
> I **wouldn't** …
>
> **Necessity**
> I **have to** get a visa.
> I **don't have to** …
> I **must** …

2 See page 143 for a list of tenses and verb forms.

3 Prepositions with time phrases

> **Seasons**
> in spring
> in summer
> in autumn
> in winter
>
> **Days of the week**
> on Monday
> on Tuesday
>
> **Events**
> after class
> before class
>
> **Time**
> at 4 o'clock
> until 4 o'clock

Key vocabulary

Nouns
advice
back pocket
camping gear
camping trip
cash
clothes
clothing
credit card
father
ferry
friend
health
health insurance
hitchhiking
kind
luggage
medicine
money
money belt
passport
penknife
place
plane ticket
shorts
sleeping bag
swimwear
tent
thing
travel document
traveller's cheques
trip

vaccination
visa
wallet

Verbs
book
bring
carry
check
find out
going to
join
pack
plan
stay
travel
wander
want

Adverb
already

Modals
had better
have to
must
ought to
should
shouldn't
would

Question words and phrases
how long …?
how many …?
what kinds …?
what other …?
what should …?
what shouldn't …?
what time …?
which tour …?

Pronoun
yourself

Preposition
until

Other words
a lot of
lots of
other
too many

Expressions
What do you think?
I've thought of that.
Why not?

Not at all!

> Making requests with imperatives and modals
> Making complaints
> Apologising and making promises

1 What was that?

Pedro is having trouble getting to sleep.
Listen to five noises which are keeping him awake.
What do you think is happening?
Discuss with a partner.

A: It sounds like some kind of machine.
B: I think it sounds like someone drilling
    in the street.

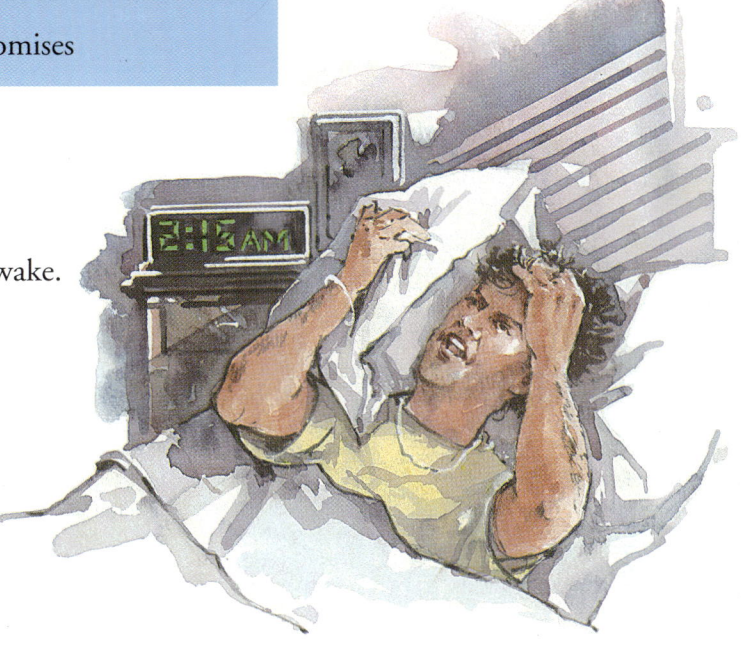

2 Conversation

1 Match each request
with the correct
response below.

a   Would you mind turning down the radio,
André? It's very loud.

b   Hey, Yoko! Could you move your car?
It's blocking my drive.

c   Would you mind not smoking here?
This is a no-smoking section.

d   Please don't leave the door open. It's
really cold outside.

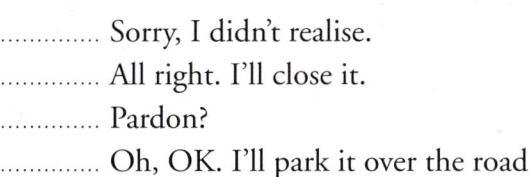

.... Sorry, I didn't realise.
.... All right. I'll close it.
.... Pardon?
.... Oh, OK. I'll park it over the road.

2 Now listen and check. Then practise with a partner.

3 Grammar focus: Requests with imperatives and modals ▭

Turn the TV **down**.	**Can** you **turn** the TV **down**?
Leave the door **open**.	**Could** you **leave** the door **open**, please?
Please **keep** the noise **down**.	**Would** you please **keep** the noise **down**?
Move your car, please.	**Would** you **mind moving** your car?
Please **don't park** here.	**Would** you **mind not parking** here, please?

1 Match each request with any suitable responses. Then compare with a partner and practise.

a Would you mind posting these letters for me?

b Excuse me. Could you move your bag, please?

c Would you mind not smoking here?

d Please try to come to class on time.

.... I'm sorry. I won't be late again. I promise!

.... OK. I'll go outside.

.... Not at all. I'll do it when I go into town this afternoon.

.... No problem!

.... Sorry. I didn't know it was bothering you.

.... I'm sorry, but it's not mine.

2 Pair work

Now take turns making the requests again. This time give your own responses.

3 Use these cues to make requests. Then compare with a partner.

a ... (lend) me some money?

b ... (get) me a cup of coffee?

c ... (open) the window.

d ... (turn) off the light?

e ... (help) me move to my new flat tomorrow?

f ... (take) your feet off my chair.

g ... (blow) smoke in my face.

4 Pronunciation: Weak forms 📼

1 Listen to the weak forms in these requests.

Could you pass me my bag?   **Would you** turn on the heating?
Could you put that away?   **Would you** turn off the video?
  /kədʒə/   /wədʒə/

2 *Pair work*

Take turns making the requests you wrote in Exercise 3.3 and giving responses.
Pay attention to weak forms.

5 No problem!

1 Think of six interesting or unusual
requests you want to make to other students
and the teacher.

2 *Class activity*

Go around the class and make your requests.
How many people accepted and how many refused?

Accepting a request	*Refusing a request*
Of course!	I'm afraid not.
Certainly!	I'm afraid I can't.
Not at all.	I'm sorry, but I'm busy at the moment.
OK. I'll do that.	I'd rather not.
All right.	What? You must be joking!

6 Listening 📼

Listen to the requests and choose the correct response.

a .... Yes, in a minute.   d .... Oh, of course.
  .... Yes, it is.   .... Yours or mine?
b .... Yes, it's very loud.   e .... No, thanks.
  .... All right.   .... Sorry, I'm using it.
c .... Of course.   f .... Oh, I'm sorry.
  .... Oh, sorry.   .... I am, too.

7 Word power: Two-part verbs

1 Which nouns from the list on the right can be used with these two-part verbs?
There may be more than one. Compare with a partner.

a hang up .... the books
b pick up .... the cat
c put away .... your cigarette
d put on .... your coat
e put out .... the tap
f take off .... the light
g take out .... the phone
h tidy up .... your clothes
i turn down .... the room
j turn off .... the radio
k turn on .... a record
l turn up .... your shoes

2 Pair work

Now make requests using four
of the verbs above.

8 Snapshot

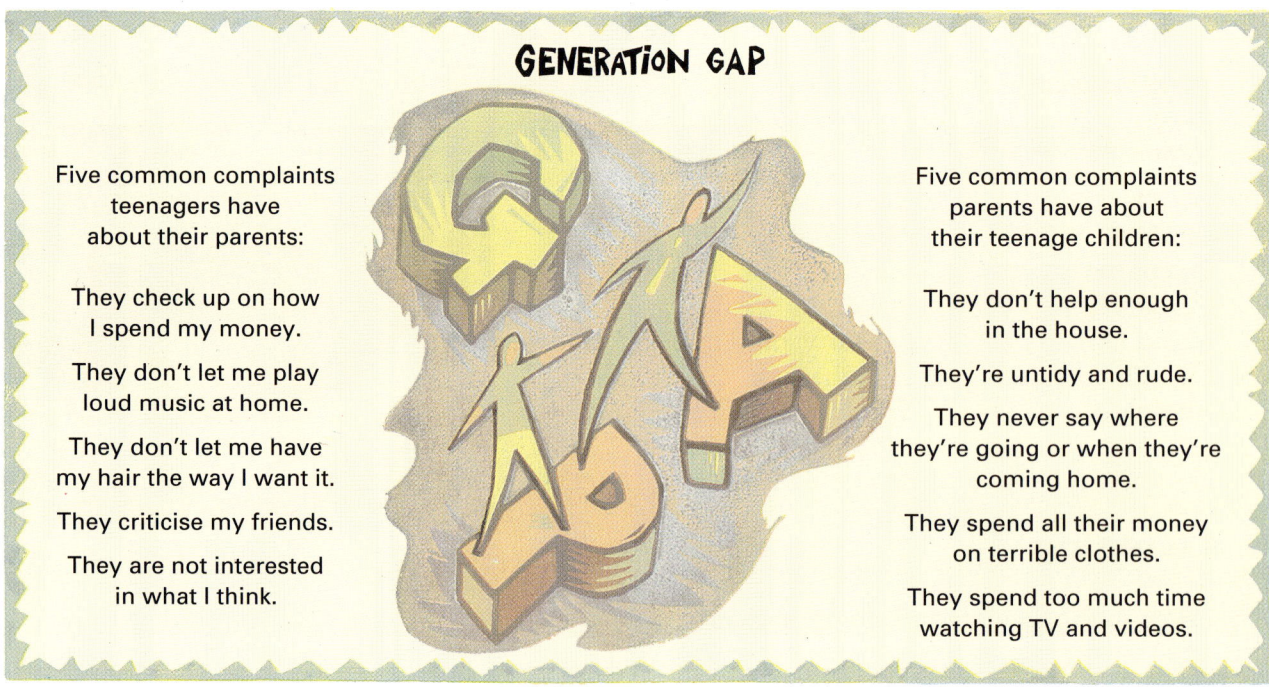

GENERATION GAP

Five common complaints
teenagers have
about their parents:

They check up on how
I spend my money.

They don't let me play
loud music at home.

They don't let me have
my hair the way I want it.

They criticise my friends.

They are not interested
in what I think.

Five common complaints
parents have about
their teenage children:

They don't help enough
in the house.

They're untidy and rude.

They never say where
they're going or when they're
coming home.

They spend all their money
on terrible clothes.

They spend too much time
watching TV and videos.

Discussion

Do you have any of the same complaints about your parents/children?
Which complaints do you think are the most important? the least important?
What is your most serious complaint about your parents/children?

9 Making complaints 📼

1 Listen to how we make complaints and respond to them.

Making a complaint
You're late! I've been waiting for an hour.
This library book was due back yesterday.

Apologising and explaining
Look, I'm sorry. I missed the bus.
Oh, sorry. I didn't realise it was overdue.

Making a complaint
Excuse me, but your car is blocking my drive.
I think you've given me the wrong change.

Apologising and offering to do something
I'm really sorry. I'll move it right away.
Sorry. Let me check the bill again.

2 Now choose the best response for each complaint. Then compare with a partner and practise them.

Complaints

a Have you forgotten? I asked you to return my book to the library.
b Remember you still owe me £20.
c I need my cassette player back. Have you finished with it?
d I waited for you at the cinema last night, but you didn't show up. What happened?

Responses

.... Sorry, they weren't there.

.... Oh, I got there late, and you had already gone. I'm really sorry.

.... Gosh, I'm sorry. Could I give them to you tomorrow?

.... Oh, I'm sorry. Can I write you a cheque?

.... Oh, it's upstairs. I'll go and get it. Sorry.

.... Oh, sorry. I completely forgot about it. I'll take it back today.

10 And another thing ...

1 Think of four things you want to complain to people about and write down each complaint.

You never give back the books you borrow.

2 **Class activity**

Now take turns complaining.
The other students respond.

11 Listening 📼

Listen to three people complaining. What are the excuses?

a .... Kim's car broke down.
   .... The traffic was bad.

b .... The restaurant is short of staff.
   .... The waiter is new to the job.

c .... Bob bakes delicious biscuits.
   .... There wasn't anything else to eat.

12 Reading: Letters to the editor

1 Read these letters to a newspaper.

June 16

Waiting Forever

The other day I was waiting for a No. 2 bus and it didn't come for over an hour. This is the second time this month it's happened to me. And another thing. The bus drivers are really rude these days. They don't wait for people to sit down before they start the bus. What does the bus company have to say about this?

Fed Up

1

Noise Pollution

I go to the parks to relax and watch the birds. But these days the parks are full of people playing loud music. Why doesn't the Council stop people playing portable stereos in public so the rest of us can enjoy some peace and quiet?

Disappointed

2

Bad Marks for the Post Office

I'd like to complain about the bad service in the post office lately. Yesterday I queued for 25 minutes to buy a stamp. Then the clerk was very rude when I gave him a £20 note for a 20p stamp. Doesn't the post office train its staff to be polite?

Angry taxpayer

3

2 Which letters from June 16th are these replies to?

No answer

I've had the same problem as your reader of June 16th. I called the post office last week and waited nearly ten minutes for an answer. And another thing, my post always comes late these days!

Annoyed customer

a

Save the Beaches

I agree with your reader of June 16th. The noise at the beach is terrible, too. I hate going there nowadays. Why don't people use personal stereos?

Unhappy

b

13 Writing: A letter to the editor

1 **Pair work**

Write a letter of complaint to a newspaper about a problem in your town.

What is the problem?
Where is it? What happens?
Why does it bother you?
What should someone do about it?

2 **Class activity**

Put your letters on the board.
Which ones do you agree with?
Which are the worst problems?

INTERCHANGE 6: THAT'S NO EXCUSE!

Find out how good you are at giving excuses. Student A look at page 129 and Student B at page 131.

Unit summary

Key vocabulary

Nouns
afternoon
bill
book
car
cassette player
cat
chair
change
cheque
cigarette
coat
cover
door
drive
face
feet
garden
letter
library
light
machine
mess
noise
no-smoking section
phone
portable stereo
radio
record
room
rubbish
shoe
smoke
tap
tennis racquet
tie
toy
TV
video

Verbs
block
blow
borrow
bother
check
drill
lend
mind
move
owe
park
pass
post
promise
queue
realise
return
smoke
wait

Two-part verbs
hang up
keep down
leave open
pick up
put away
put out
take back
take off
take out
tidy up
turn off
turn on
turn up

Adjectives
due back
late
loud
open
overdue
rude
torn
wrong

Adverbs
again
completely
like
on time
right away
still

Prepositions
about
outside
upstairs

Other words
mine
some kind of
someone

Expressions
Excuse me.
By the way, …
Of course.
Certainly.
OK. I'll do that.
I'm afraid I can't.
I'm sorry, but I'm busy at the moment.
I'd rather not.
What? You must be joking!
Pardon?
Gosh!
What happened?

4-6 Review

1 Listening 🔲

1 Listen to the Seasoned Chef describing a favourite summer recipe on his radio programme *Cooking for all Seasons*. Tick the ingredients that you hear.

.... curry powder
.... celery
.... water
.... lettuce
.... mayonnaise
.... milk
.... peanuts
.... pepper
.... rice
.... walnuts

2 Listen again and write down the recipe. Use these words: *boil*, *chop*, *add* and *mix*. Compare with a partner.

2 Food for thought

1 *Pair work*

Take turns asking these questions. If you answer 'Yes', describe what happened.

Have you ever …

baked a cake?	not had enough money to pay a bill in a restaurant?
made rice salad?	sent back a dish you ordered in a restaurant?
drunk mint tea?	been to a barbecue?
tried snails?	been to a Mexican restaurant?
cooked chicken curry?	cooked a terrible meal for friends?
eaten brains?	eaten in a Japanese restaurant?

2 *Class activity*

Ask your partner to tell you an interesting experience she/he has had with food or restaurants. Tell the rest of the class like this.

> Anna went to San Francisco last year. She ordered a bowl of onion soup in a restaurant, but she sent it back to the kitchen because there was a snail in it!

3 Conversation: The weekend

Pair work

Talk about your weekend plans.
What are you going to do?

A: Do you have any plans for the weekend?
B: Yes, I'm going to be really busy.
A: Me too. What are you doing?
B: Well, on Saturday morning I'm …
   How about you?
A: On Saturday I'm …
B: Sounds fun! What about Sunday?
A: I'm … And you?
B: …Well, have a nice weekend!
A: …

4 On the road

1 Group work

Your friends are planning to make a long
car trip on their next holiday.

What plans do they need to make?
How many suggestions can you think of?
Use *had better, must, ought to, should*
and *shouldn't*.

You must plan your trip.

You'd better take some road maps.

You should put petrol in your car.

You shouldn't take too many clothes.

2 Class activity

Compare your suggestions.

5 Sorry to remind you, but …

1 Pair work

Cover your partner's information.

Student A: Complain to your partner about these things:

– Your partner has not returned your tennis racquet.
– Your partner is playing a cassette very loudly. You are trying to study.
– Your partner has been on the telephone for twenty minutes. You need to make a phone call.
– Your partner borrowed your typewriter. You need to use it.

Student B: Listen to your partner's complaints. Apologise and make suitable responses.

What on earth is that?

Countables and uncountables: *a, some*
Gerunds and infinitives after prepositions

1 Snapshot

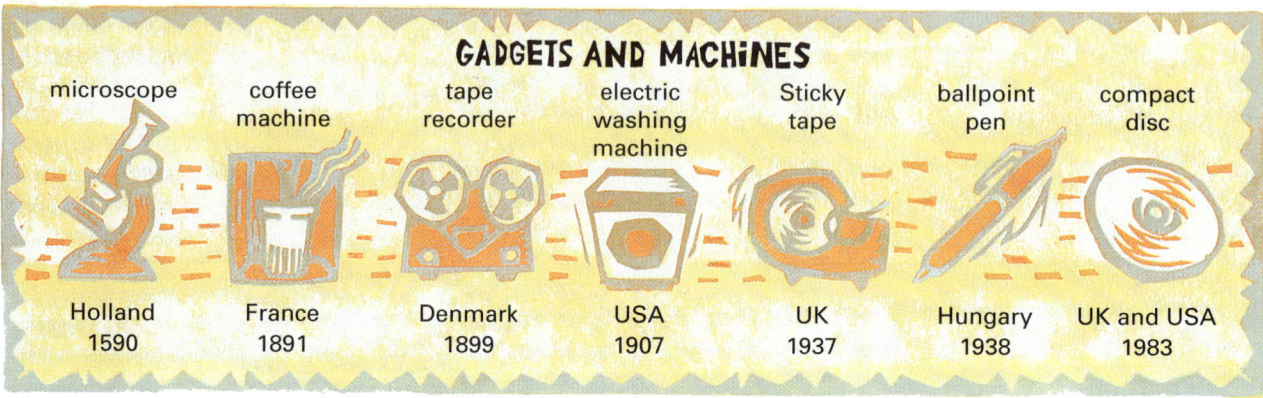

GADGETS AND MACHINES

microscope	coffee machine	tape recorder	electric washing machine	Sticky tape	ballpoint pen	compact disc
Holland 1590	France 1891	Denmark 1899	USA 1907	UK 1937	Hungary 1938	UK and USA 1983

Discussion

Which do you think are the three most important inventions in the last 50 years?
What are the three most useful gadgets in your home?
What is the most useless gadget you've ever owned?

2 Conversation

1 Listen.

Customer: What on earth is that?
Shop assistant: That? Oh, it's called a Musical Finder. It's a wonderful gadget.
Customer: What's it for?
Shop assistant: It's used for finding things that you always lose! It's amazing. Look! You clip it onto your glasses at night, then in the morning you just clap twice and it plays a tune to tell you where they are! Listen!
Customer: I don't wear glasses, but thanks anyway.

2 Listen to the rest of the conversation.

What other things can you use the Musical Finder for?
What does the customer want to use it for?

3 **Word power:** Countable and uncountable nouns

1 Write these countable nouns under the headings below
and add one more word to each list.

broom   paper clip   ruler   tin opener
lighter   penknife   stapler   vacuum cleaner

Office supplies	*Gadgets*	*Cleaning equipment*
....	....	....
....	....	....
....	....	....
....	....	....

2 Write these uncountable nouns under the headings
below and add one more word to each list.

detergent   milk   soap   tea
glue   polish   sticky tape   water

Office supplies	*Drinks*	*Cleaning supplies*
....	....	....
....	....	....
....	....	....
....	....	....

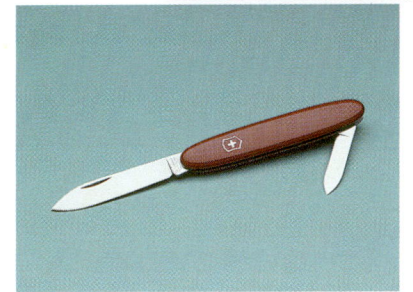

4 **Grammar focus:** Gerunds or infinitives after a preposition 🎞

Gerunds	Infinitives
It's used **for finding** things.	It's used **to find** things.
You can use it **for making** things.	You can use it **to make** things.

1 Complete the phrases in column A with suitable information in column B.

A

a You can use scissors
b You can use a corkscrew
c Glue is used
d A blender is used
e You can use pliers
f A ruler is used

B

.... to open bottles (with).
.... to open tins (with).
.... for measuring things (with).
.... for cutting paper or cloth (with).
.... to make drinks (with).
.... to stick things together (with).
.... for pulling out nails (with).
.... to sharpen pencils (with).

2 Write four questions about things in your home.
Then take turns asking your questions.

What is a vacuum cleaner used for?

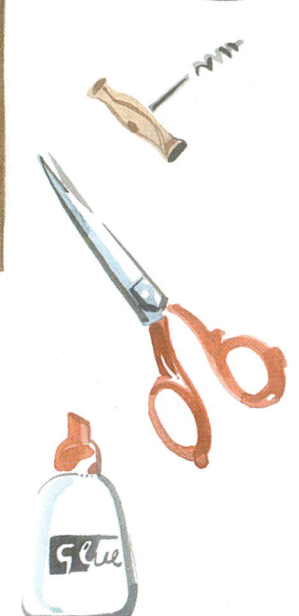

5 Pronunciation: Stress in compound nouns

1   In compound nouns, the first noun receives greater stress than the second.
    Listen and practise.

    CD player   **coffee** pot   **motor**bike   **paper** clip   **pen**knife   **tin** opener

2   *Pair work*

    List six more compound nouns for household items. Then say what they are used for.

6 Listening

1   Listen to people talking about
    three of these gadgets.
    Number the pictures 1 to 3
    in the order you hear them.

2   Listen again.
    What is each gadget used for?

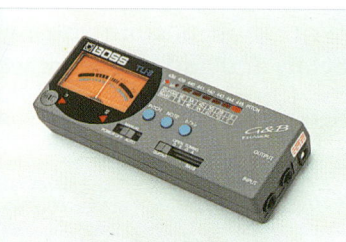

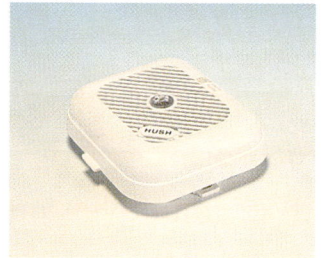

7 Things in common

1   *Group work*

    Find groups of words that have something in common. You can use the same words in more than one
    group. Make lists.

    Chopsticks, a fork and a knife are all used for eating.

    | a cassette tape | an envelope | a paper clip | soap | a television |
    | a CD player | a fork | a radio | a stamp | a video |
    | chopsticks | glue | a record | stationery | |
    | detergent | a knife | shampoo | sticky tape | |

    Useful expressions

    ... are all used to make things.   ... are all used for making things.
    ... are all made of ...   ... are all kept in the ...

2   Now compare your lists with another group of students.

3   *Class activity*

    Who found the most groups of words? What were they?

8 Conversation

1 Listen.

Saleswoman: Good afternoon. Can I help you?
Customer: Something's wrong with this watch.
Saleswoman: What's the problem?
Customer: Well, it's stopped.
Saleswoman: Oh? How long have you had it?
Customer: About a year.
Saleswoman: Right. Let me have a look. Oh, the
             battery needs changing and I think it
             needs to be cleaned. That's all.
Customer: Well, that's a relief!

2 *Pair work*

Now close your books and practise
the conversation again.

9 Grammar focus: Gerunds and infinitives

Gerunds	Infinitives
The watch **needs cleaning**.	The watch **needs to be cleaned**.
The battery **needs changing**.	The battery **needs to be changed**.

1 Read about these problems and choose suitable suggestions.
Then compare with a partner and practise.

a These trousers are too long.
b These boots look terrible!
c My Walkman won't work.
d The lock on the door is broken.
e My car sounds funny.
f My suit looks awful!
g My hair is too long.

.... It needs to be repaired.

.... Maybe the batteries need changing.

.... They need to be shortened.

.... It probably needs servicing.

.... It needs cutting.

.... They need to be polished.

.... It needs dry cleaning.

2 *Pair work*

Now look at these problems and make suggestions.

a My motorbike won't start.
b I can't get the video to work.
c This room is a mess!
d I dropped my alarm clock and now it doesn't ring.
e The manager spilled coffee on her dress.

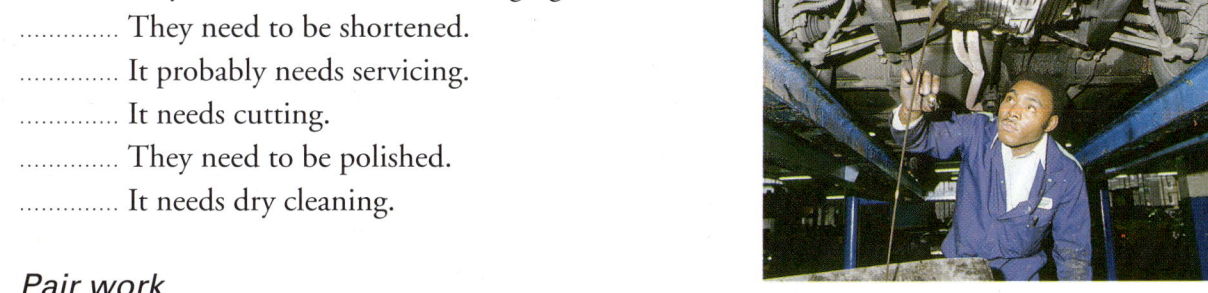

10 Listening

Listen to two customers describing problems with things they've bought.
What is the problem? What needs doing?
Make notes.

11 'Needs some attention'

1 Pair work

Look at these pictures of some flats and one of the rooms.
How many problems can you find? What needs to be done?

Useful vocabulary

Nouns	Verbs
curtains	clean
dustbin	cut
grass and weeds	mend
street light	pick up
window	repair

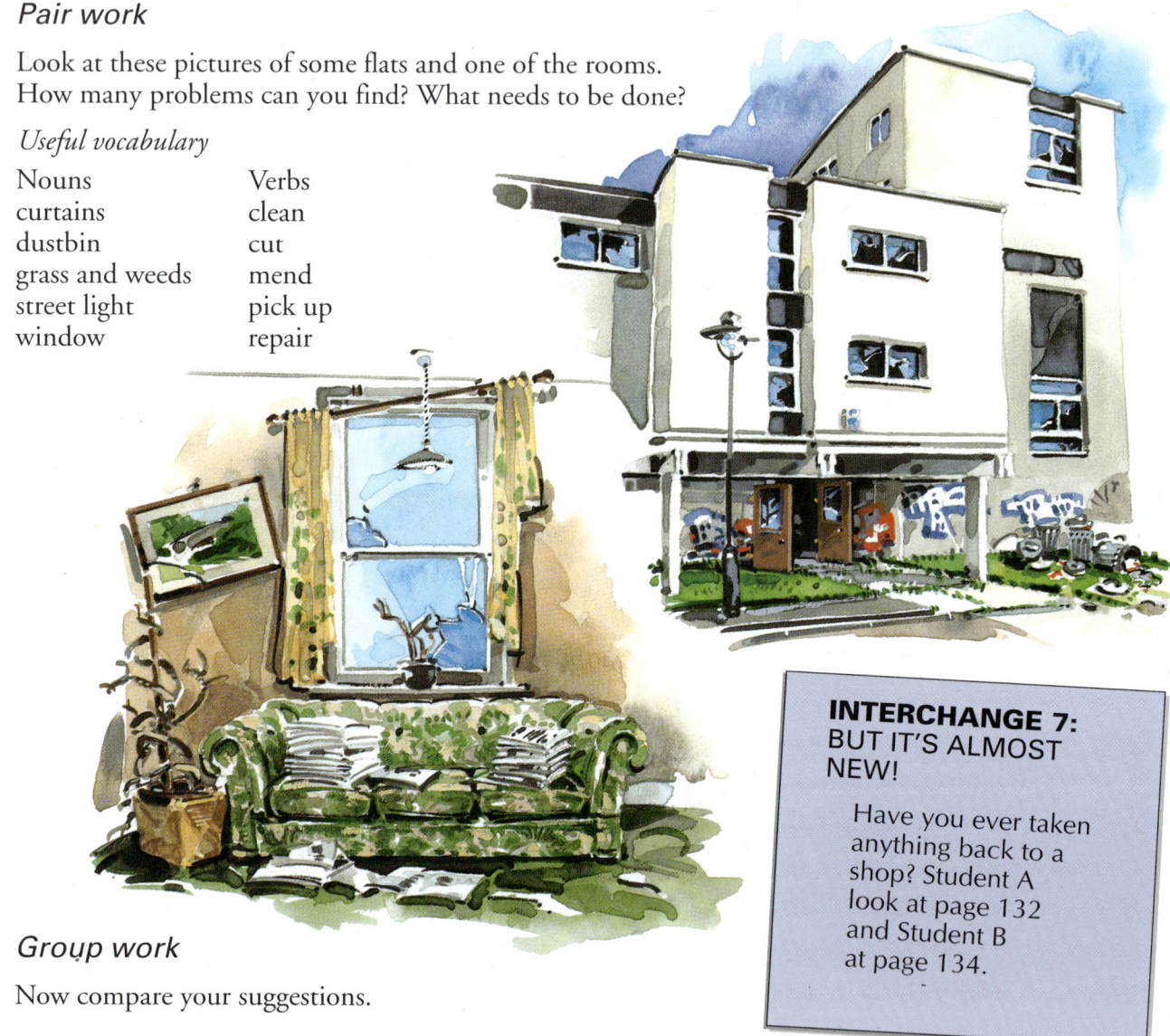

2 Group work

Now compare your suggestions.

INTERCHANGE 7: BUT IT'S ALMOST NEW!

Have you ever taken anything back to a shop? Student A look at page 132 and Student B at page 134.

12 Writing

Someone is coming to your house to repair something. You won't be at home.
Write a note describing the problem.

> The refrigerator isn't working properly. Would you mind having a look at it? I think the temperature control needs checking. It doesn't seem to work. It's too cold and everything freezes! Thanks.

13 Reading: Advertisements

1   Read these advertisements for unusual gadgets and match each one with a picture.

1    2    3    4

a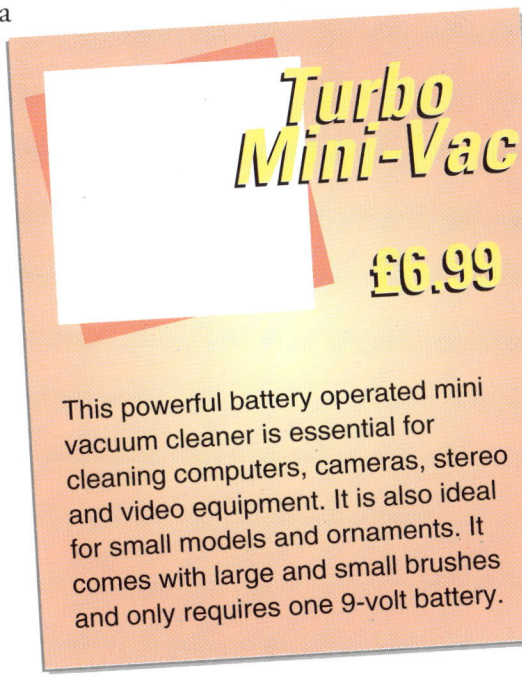

Turbo Mini-Vac

£6.99

This powerful battery operated mini vacuum cleaner is essential for cleaning computers, cameras, stereo and video equipment. It is also ideal for small models and ornaments. It comes with large and small brushes and only requires one 9-volt battery.

b

Can Crusher

£10.99

Easily the best way to reduce aluminium cans to 20% of their size ready for recycling. This wall mounted device (screws included) has a soft grip handle and simple lever action, making it easy and safe to use.

c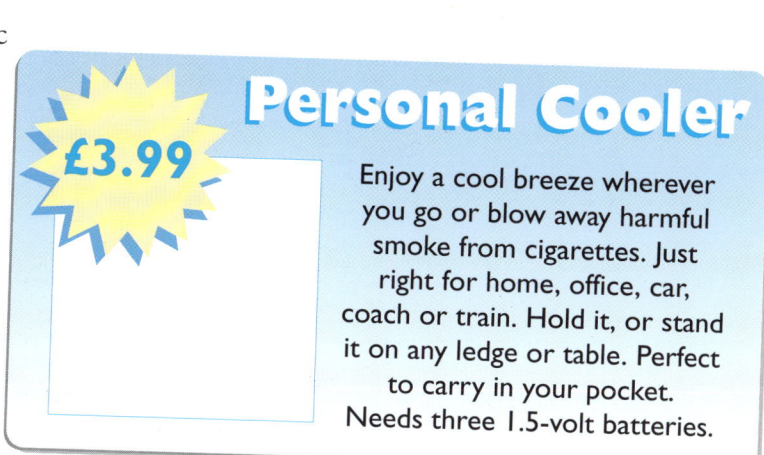

Personal Cooler

£3.99

Enjoy a cool breeze wherever you go or blow away harmful smoke from cigarettes. Just right for home, office, car, coach or train. Hold it, or stand it on any ledge or table. Perfect to carry in your pocket. Needs three 1.5-volt batteries.

d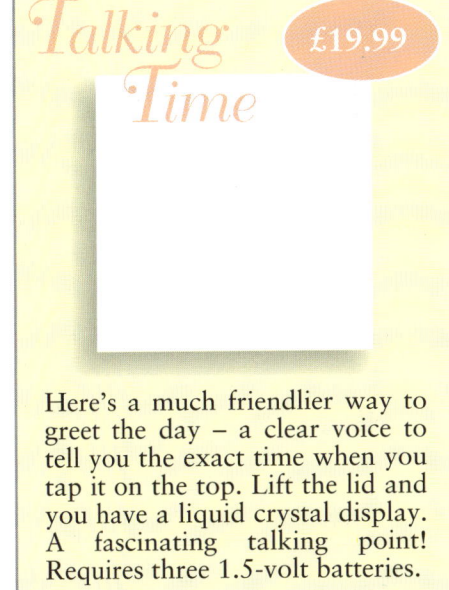

Talking Time

£19.99

Here's a much friendlier way to greet the day – a clear voice to tell you the exact time when you tap it on the top. Lift the lid and you have a liquid crystal display. A fascinating talking point! Requires three 1.5-volt batteries.

2   Which of these gadgets would you buy? Why?

3   **Pair work**

Think up an unusual gadget that you'd like to have. What is it for? How does it work? Where can you use it?

Unit summary

Key vocabulary

Nouns
battery
blender
boots
broom
cassette tape
CD player
chopsticks
cleaning supplies
cloth
corkscrew
curtains
detergent
dustbin
envelope
fork
gadget
glasses
glue
grass
invention
knife
lighter
lock
manager
milk
motorbike
nail
office supplies
paper
paper clip
penknife
pliers
polish
refrigerator
ruler
scissors
shampoo
soap
stamp
stapler
stationery
street light
tape
tea
television
trousers
tune
vacuum cleaner
VCR
watch
water
weeds

Verbs
break
change
clap
clean
clip
cut
drop

dry clean
keep
measure
mend
pick up
polish
pull out
repair
service
sharpen
shorten
spill
stick
stop
use

Adjectives
amazing
funny
long
terrible
terrific
useful
useless
wonderful

Adverbs
now
probably

Other words
all
most
twice

Expressions
What on earth is that?
What's it for?
Can I help you?
Let me have a look.
That's all!
That's a relief!
Thanks, anyway.

Unit 8

Let's celebrate!

Relative clauses of time
Adverbial clauses of time

1 Snapshot

HOLIDAYS AND FESTIVALS

January 1st	New Year's Day: This is a national holiday in many countries.
January or February	Chinese New Year: Chinese people celebrate with firecrackers and lion dances.
May 5th	Children's Day: Japanese families put up coloured streamers shaped like fish in honour of their children.
November 5th	Guy Fawkes' Night: People in England have bonfires and fireworks to remember the death of Guy Fawkes, who tried to blow up the Houses of Parliament.
December 25th	Christmas: People in many countries decorate Christmas trees and give each other presents.

Discussion

Which of these holidays do you have in your country?
What other special days do you have? What's your favourite holiday or festival?

2 Word power

1   Add these words to
the word map.

anniversary
birthday
cake
cards
dancing
fireworks
flowers
parade
presents
roast turkey
special sweets
wedding

2   Now add four more words
to the map. Then compare
with a partner.

Activities
....
....
....
....

Things we give
and receive
....
....
....
....

Celebrations

Special food and
drink
....
....
....
....

Special occasions
....
....
....
....

3 Conversation

Listen.

Tina: Hey, Mark! Did you know it's St Patrick's Day
next week?
Mark: Oh? What happens then?
Tina: Well, it's a day when Irish people always have
lots of parades and parties, and everyone wears
green and a shamrock! Would you like to
come to a St Patrick's Day party?
Mark: Yes, I'd love to.
Tina: Good! Remember to wear something green!
Mark: OK. Maybe I'll wear that green tie you gave
me for my birthday!

4 Grammar focus: Relative clauses of time

> March 17th is **the day when** the Irish remember St Patrick.
> August is **the month when** many Europeans go on holiday.
> October is **the month when** Canadians celebrate Thanksgiving.

1 How much do you know about these special days? Complete the sentences in column A with information in column B. Then compare with a partner.

A   B
a February is the month when   .... Brazilians celebrate Carnival.
b April Fool's Day is the day when   .... people like to have parties.
c May Day is the day when   .... the French celebrate their revolution.
d The Fourth of July is the day when   .... people play tricks on friends.
e July 14th is the day when   .... people in many countries honour workers.
f New Year's Eve is the night when   .... Americans celebrate their independence.

2 Now complete these clauses with information of your own.

Winter is a season when …
Valentine's Day is a day when …
Spring is a time of year when …
Mother's Day is the day when …
July is a month when …
A birthday is a day when …
A wedding anniversary is a time when …

3 Now write four more sentences
like these about special days and times.
Then compare with a partner.

5 Listening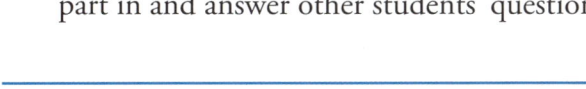

Nick has just returned from Jordan.
Listen to him talking about Ramadan,
a special time in the Islamic year.
Take notes.

What is Ramadan?
How long does it last?
When do people eat during Ramadan?
What happens at the end of Ramadan?

6 Once a year

1 Pair work

Take turns asking and answering these
questions, and ask questions of your own.

Is there an interesting festival in your area?
When is it?
How do people celebrate it?
Do you eat any special food?
What else do people do?
What do you like most about it?

2 Class activity

Give a short talk about a festival you have taken
part in and answer other students' questions.

7 Writing

1 What do you do on your birthday?
What usually happens?
Make notes and then write about
it like this.

On the evening of my birthday
I often have a party for my friends.
I usually cook something special
and …

2 Pair work

Read each other's compositions.
Do you have any questions?

8 Conversation

1 Listen.

Charles: You look beautiful in that wedding dress, Juliette, but what's this other wedding picture?

Juliette: Well, in France, when you get married, you often have two weddings.

Charles: Two? Why's that?

Juliette: You see, before you marry in church, you have a civil wedding in the Town Hall.

Charles: I still don't see why you need two weddings!

Juliette: Well, the religious ceremony is optional, but you have to have the civil wedding.

Charles: And what about receptions? Do you have two of them?

Juliette: I'm afraid not! You usually have the reception after the religious wedding.

2 Now listen to the rest of the conversation and take notes.

How many people were at Juliette's reception?
Who gave speeches?
What happened at the reception?

9 Pronunciation: Stress and rhythm in sentences

1 In a sentence the words with the most important information are usually stressed. Listen to these sentences and then practise them.

In France you have a civil wedding before you marry in church.

The civil wedding is always in the Town Hall.

2 Now mark the stresses in these sentences. Then listen and check with a partner, and practise the sentences.

When people have birthdays, they usually get presents from friends.

June is a month when many young people like to get married.

When people get married they often have a reception.

Most couples live together after they get married.

10 Grammar focus: Adverbial clauses of time 📼

> **Before Western couples get married**, they usually go out together a lot.
> **After the wedding ceremony finishes**, there is usually a reception.
> **When a bride marries in a church**, she often wears a white dress.

Look at this information about weddings in Britain. Complete the clauses in column A
with the information in column B.

A	B
a Before a man and a woman get married,	.... the newlyweds usually live together.
b Before the man gets married,	.... she may wear a white wedding dress.
c When the woman gets engaged,	.... they usually go out together for a year or so.
d When the woman gets married,	.... his friends often give him an all male party.
e After the couple gets married,	.... she usually wears a ring.
f After they return from their honeymoon,	.... there's usually a wedding reception.

11 Marriage customs

1 Group work

Talk about marriage customs in your country. Ask these questions and others of your own.

How old are people usually when they get married?
Is there an engagement period? How long is it?
Who pays for the wedding?
Who is invited?
Where is the wedding ceremony usually held?

What happens during the ceremony?
What do the bride and groom usually wear?
Is there a reception after the ceremony?
What type of food is served at the reception?
What kinds of gifts do people usually give?

> **INTERCHANGE 8:**
> ONCE IN A BLUE MOON
>
> How do other people in your class celebrate special events? Find out on page 133.

2 Group work

Do you know any marriage customs in other countries?
Tell other students what you know.

12 Reading: Customs round the world

Read about these unusual customs. Then find the best title for each passage.

.... A Day for Children   .... Everything New for New Year

.... Choosing the Right Clothes   .... Shouting 'Goodbye' to Winter

.... Blessing the Animals   .... A Special Kind of Meal

a

In the evening of February 3rd, people in Japanese families take one dried bean for each year of their age and throw the beans on the floor, shouting 'Good luck in! Evil spirits out!' This is known as 'Setsubun', a time to celebrate the end of winter and the beginning of spring.

b

Before the Chinese New Year, many Chinese families burn the picture of their kitchen god, Tsao Chen, to bring good luck. When New Year's Day comes, they put up a new picture of Tsao Chen on the wall.

c

When British women get married, they sometimes follow an old custom in choosing what to wear for their wedding day. The custom says the bride must wear 'something old, something new, something borrowed, and something blue.' This is to bring good luck.

d

Before Lent (a time on the Christian calendar), the people of Ponti, Italy, eat an omelette made with 1000 eggs. People must not eat animal products during Lent, so they try to use up these things before Lent begins.

e

When winter ends in the Czech Republic, children make a straw man called 'Smrt', which is a figure of death. Then they burn it or throw it in the river. After they destroy it, they carry flowers home to show the arrival of spring.

f

January 17th is St Anthony's Day in Mexico. It's a day when people bring their animals to church. But before the animals go into the church, the people dress them up in flowers and ribbons. This ceremony is to protect people's animals.

Unit summary

Grammar

1 Cardinal and ordinal numbers

Cardinal	Ordinal
one	first
two	second
three	third
four	fourth
five	fifth
six	sixth
seven	seventh
eight	eighth
nine	ninth
ten	tenth
eleven	eleventh
twelve	twelfth

2 Adverbs of frequency

People always …
usually …
often …
sometimes …
occasionally …
hardly ever …
never …

Key vocabulary

Nouns
activity
anniversary
birthday
bride
cake
card
ceremony
couple
custom
dancing
engagement
festival
fireworks
flower
gift
groom
holiday
honeymoon
independence
marriage
month
newlyweds
occasion
parade
period
present
reception
revolution
roast turkey
season
sweet
trick
wedding
worker

**Months of
the year**
January
February
March
April
May
June
July
August
September
October
November
December

Verbs
celebrate
get engaged
get married
happen
hold
honour
invite
receive
remember

Adjectives
beautiful
religious
special

Colours
black
blue
brown
green
grey
orange
pink
purple
red
white
yellow
light green
dark green

Adverb
during

Question phrases
how old …?
what else …?
what kind …?
what type …?

Other words
a year or so
each other
most
something
together

Expression
I'm afraid not.

Back to the future!

Comparing past, present and future   Modals
First and second conditionals

1 Snapshot

PAST, PRESENT AND FUTURE

People who ...
would like to travel back to the past: 30%
would like to travel into the future: 67%
think we were better off in the past: 26%
think we will be better off in the future: 35%
would like to live to be a hundred years old: 50%
have booked flights to the moon: 92 000
think they look younger than they are: 57%

Discussion

Would you like to travel in time? Which way and how far?
Do you think people were better off in the past than now?
Will we be better off in the future?
Would you book a flight to the moon?

2 Conversation

1 Listen.

Cindy: Gran, do you think
                people were better off in the
                past than they are now?
Grandmother: Well, yes, in some ways,
                because people didn't use to
                rush around like they do today.
Cindy: No, I suppose not.
Grandmother: But there are some things
                I like better today.
Cindy: Really? Like what?
Grandmother: Well, I love my new car!
                And I couldn't live without
                my computer! These
                computer games are the
                best fun I've ever had!

2 Listen to the rest of the conversation.
What does Cindy like about the old days?

3 **Grammar focus:** Time contrasts 🔲

Past	Present	Future
In the past, people **didn't travel** so much.	These days, people **travel** a lot more.	Soon, people **will travel** to other planets.
Families **used to stay** at home more.	Nowadays, they **don't stay** at home so much.	In fifty years, more people **may work** at home.
Fifty years ago, people **lived** to about sixty.	Today, people **live** to about seventy-five.	In the future, people **may live** to a hundred.

1   Complete the phrases in column A with suitable information from column B.
    Then compare with a partner.

A

a About a hundred years ago,
b Before jet travel,
c In most offices today,
d In many cities around the world,
e In the next fifty years,
f In two hundred years,

B

.... pollution is a serious problem.

.... the world's supply of oil may run out.

.... cities began to build the first underground systems.

.... it took more than twelve hours to fly from New York to Paris.

.... there will probably be cities on the moon.

.... people work about a forty hour week.

2   Now finish these sentences with your own ideas and compare with a partner.

'Five years ago, I …'   'Now, I …'   'In five years, I'll …'

4 **Pronunciation:** Pitch 🔲

1   Listen to how the first phrase has lower pitch than the main clause in these sentences.

In the past, people didn't travel so much.

These days, people travel a lot more.

Soon, people will travel to other planets.

2   Listen and practise the sentences you completed in Exercise 3.1.

3   Now complete the phrases in column A in Exercise 3.1 with information of your own.
    Then practise them with a partner. Pay attention to pitch.

5 Listening 📼

1 Listen to these statements. Tick if the speaker is describing
something in the past, present or future.

	Past	Present	Future		Past	Present	Future
a	....	....	....	e	....	....	....
b	....	....	....	f	....	....	....
c	....	....	....	g	....	....	....
d	....	....	....	h	....	....	....

6 Changing times

Group work

Talk about how things have changed.
Choose two of these topics or other topics of
your own and discuss the questions below.

Clothing   Housing
Education   Transport
Entertainment   Work
Health

What was it like a hundred years ago?
What's it like now?
What will it be like in a hundred years?

7 Writing

1 Write about your hopes for the future.
(Don't put your name on your paper.)

In ten years I hope I'll be a successful actress.
I'm sure I'll be famous and I'll star in films
and on TV. I'll probably…

2 *Class activity*

Pass your compositions around the class.
Read another student's paper.
Can you guess who wrote it?

8 Conversation

1 Listen.

Adam: You know, I really should start doing some exercises. I'm so unfit!
Ben: Yes, me too. And I know if I start jogging to work, I can save about £50 a month in fares.
Adam: Fantastic! The trouble is, though, if I start doing exercises, I'm sure I'll eat more and then I might put on weight.
Ben: Yes, and if I jog to work, I'll have to get up earlier.
Adam: Well, if we started all this next month, we'd have time to get ready.
Ben: Yes, and if we waited till the spring, the weather might be better.
Adam: Good idea! Fancy a doughnut?

2 *Group work*

Is there anything you think you should start or stop doing? What will happen if you do?

9 Grammar focus: 1st and 2nd conditionals with modals

> **If I start doing exercises, I'll** eat more.
> **If I eat more, I might** put on weight.
> **If we started next month, we would** have time to get ready.
> **If we waited till the spring, the weather might** be better.

1 Complete the clauses in column A with information in column B. Then compare with a partner and practise them.

A

a If they ban smoking on all planes,
b If people used their cars only on weekends,
c If they build a good underground system,
d If people ate less meat,
e If cities passed laws against keeping dogs as pets,

B

.... the streets would be a lot cleaner.
.... some people will travel by train.
.... they would probably be a lot healthier.
.... there would be less pollution in cities.
.... more people might get rid of their cars.

2 *Pair work*

Now take turns and complete the clauses in column A with your own information.

10 Listening 📼

Listen to people complaining. What are they complaining about?
What laws would they like to see passed?

	Complaint	Suggested law
a	....	....
b	....	....
c	....	....

11 There should be a law against it!

1 Group work

What are some things that really annoy you?
What should be done about them? Choose three
problems and talk about them like this.

A: I wish they'd do something about the
parks in this town. People leave rubbish
all over the place. It's awful!
B: I know. I don't even like going to the
parks any more. They're just so dirty.

2 Now describe a law you would like to see passed.

If people leave rubbish in a park or public place,
they should have to work with the Council
rubbish department for a weekend and clean
up the public places.

3 Class activity

Compare your laws. Are there any you
disagree with?

12 Word power: Strong feelings

1 Look at these ways of expressing strong feelings.

People who leave rubbish around the parks really
annoy/infuriate/disgust me!
I hate/can't stand people who throw sweet wrappers
on the ground!
Bad drivers make me angry/furious/wild!
I think the new Town Hall is awful/horrible/terrible!

2 Now describe five things you feel strongly about.
Compare with a partner.

INTERCHANGE 9:
PROS AND CONS

Join the debate!
Turn to page 133 and
give your opinion
on some controversial
topics.

13 Reading: Against the law

1 Read this information about unusual laws.

d In 1949, in Illinois, USA, bird lovers tried to get a law passed to keep cats on a lead in public. However, the governor refused to pass the law. He said the problem of cats against birds was as old as time itself. If we favour cats, then we will have to decide between dogs and cats or even birds and worms.

a Sailors are not allowed to whistle on ships at sea. This is because people used to believe that whistling would bring high winds and cause danger to the ship.

b In seventeenth century Japan, it was against the law for any citizen to leave the country. Anyone who was found leaving the country or arriving from overseas without permission was sentenced to death.

e It's against the law to drive any motor vehicle except tractors on the island of Sark in the English Channel. Most of the people there use bicycles for transport.

c In Russia in the eighteenth century, it was against the law for any man to wear a beard unless he paid a special tax.

f In Venice, many people travel through the canals on gondolas. The law requires gondolas to be painted black, except for those belonging to high government officials.

2 Find nouns that mean:

having consent to do something (paragraph b): ....

money collected by the government (paragraph c): ....

a length of rope or chain to control an animal (paragraph d): ....

something that carries people from one place to another (paragraph e): ....

people who hold an office (paragraph f): ....

Unit summary

Grammar

1 Conditional clauses

> **With future reference**
> If it **rains**, we **won't go**.
> If it **rains**, I **may/might stay** at home.
> If I **see** her, I **will tell** her.
> If I **phone** him, I **could give** him the message.
>
> **With imaginary situations**
> If I **found** some money, I **would/might take** it to the police.
> If I **had** more time, I **would/might study** another language.
>
> **With imaginary situations in the past**
> If I **had found** some money, I **would/might have kept** it.
> If I **had known** you were here, I **would have phoned** you.

2 Adverbs for future time

> Soon, people will …
> Next year, …
> In a few years, …
> In the next few years, …
> Within twenty years, …
> In fifty years, …
> In the future, …
> In the next century, …
> By 2050, …

Key vocabulary

Nouns
computer
doughnut
education
fare
flight
future
ground
hour
jet
law
meat
moon
oil
park
past
plane
planet
pollution
supply
system
train

Verbs
annoy
ban
bother
can't stand

do exercises
get rid of
hate
infuriate
jog
pass
put on weight
run out
rush around
save
travel
wish

Adjectives
angry
healthy
horrible
unfit
wild

Adverbs
ago
nowadays
probably
soon
these days

Conjunction
because

Preposition
against

Other words
better off
less
any more

Expressions
I couldn't live without …
You know …
In some ways …
Like what?
No, I suppose not.
Me, too.

Review

1 What's the problem?

1 Role play

Student A is an assistant in a shop selling electrical goods. Student B is a customer who has a problem with one of the things below. The customer describes the problem and the assistant suggests what is wrong.

A: Hello. Can I help you?
B: Yes. Something's wrong with my …
A: Oh, what's the problem?
B: …
A: OK. Let me have a look at it. Perhaps … Yes, you see it's the … It needs …
B: Oh, really?
A: Yes. Can you leave it here for repair?
B: … And how much will it cost?
A: Well, it should …
B: And how long do you need to repair it?
A: I think it will take about …
Can you come back on … ?
B: … Thanks very much.
A: …

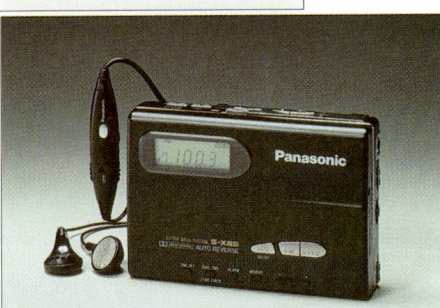

2 Now change roles and talk about another item.

---

2 Listening

1 Listen to some information about unusual marriage customs. Are the statements below true (**T**) or false (**F**)?

a When two women of a tribe in Paraguay want to marry the same man, they put on boxing gloves and fight it out.
b When a man and a woman get married in Malaysia, they eat some cooked rice the day before the wedding.
c In north-eastern India before a girl gets married, she rides through the village on a horse.
d In some parts of India when a man and a woman get married, water is poured over them.

2 Now listen again. For the statements you marked false, what is the correct information?

3   That's an interesting custom!

1   Group work

In many countries, there are interesting customs for births, marriages, the seasons, or good luck. What interesting customs do you know? Take turns talking about them like this.

When a boy wants to marry a girl in some parts of the Philippines, he stands outside her house at night and sings to her.

Others ask questions.

Why does he do that?
Is it just a village custom?
Is it common?
Do women do the same thing?

2   Class activity

Which was the most interesting custom you talked about in your group?
Tell the class about it.

4   Make your own rules!

1   Pair work

What rules would you like to see in your classroom? Think of some interesting rules for these situations.

If students …
    arrive late for class, they will have to …
    use their own language during a lesson, they must …
    miss a class, they will have to …

If a teacher …
    arrives late for class, she/he will have to …
    gives back homework late, she/he must …
    doesn't finish the lesson on time, she/he will have to …

If a student has a birthday, the class will …
If the teacher has a birthday, the students will …

2   Class activity

Compare your rules.

What do you think of him?

Describing abilities	Adjectives of personality
Short responses	Adverbs

1 Snapshot

WORK! WORK! WORK!

Some statistics

Hours worked on average per week in EC:		42
Number of foreign employees in:	Greece	25 000
	UK	820 000
	France	1 130 000
Jobs in Denmark done by women:		45%
Jobs in Europe done by 'under 25s':		17%
Most claustrophobic job:		astronaut
Most competitive job:		actor

Discussion

How do you think these facts compare with your country?
Do you think there are more or fewer foreign employees in your country?
What jobs do they do?

2 Conversation

1 Listen.

Jason: I need a holiday job.
Don: So do I. Are there any interesting jobs in the paper today?
Jason: Well, there's one here for a tour guide. But you have to work Saturdays and Sundays.
Don: I don't really want to work at weekends.
Jason: Neither do I. Oh, there's another one here for a salesperson. It's a job selling children's books.
Don: Sounds interesting.
Jason: Yes, but you need a driving licence, and I can't drive.
Don: Ah, but *I* can! What's the phone number?

2 Now listen to the phone conversation. What else does the job require?

3 **Grammar focus:** Statement and response 🔲

I can type.	**So can** I.	I can't.
I can't drive.	**Neither can** I.	Oh, I can.
I'm good at maths.	**So am** I.	I'm not.
I'm not good at languages.	**Neither am** I.	I am.
I like office work.	**So do** I.	Oh, I don't.
I don't enjoy sales work.	**Neither do** I.	Well, I do.

1   Make responses to these statements.
Then compare with a partner.

a I haven't got a driving licence.
b I'm not very good at writing reports.
c I can speak three languages.
d I don't like working overtime.
e I'm quite good at economics.
f I can't type very fast.
g I like working at weekends.

2   Now write five sentences about
yourself like the ones above.
Say them to your partner.
She/He responds.

4 **Pronunciation:** Stress in responses 🔲

1   Listen to the stressed words in these responses. Then practise them.

So can I.   **Neither** can I.
So am I.   **Neither** am I.
So do I.   **Neither** do I.

2   Now listen to the stressed words in the responses to these statements. Then practise them.

Statements	*Responses*
I don't like working on Saturdays.	Oh, **I** do!
I can't use a computer.	**I** can!
I really like studying grammar.	Well, **I** don't.

3 *Pair work*

Take turns reading the statements you wrote in Exercise 3.2 again.
Pay attention to stress in the responses.

5 Listening 📼

Listen and tick the correct response.

a .... So do I.
  .... So can I.

b .... So can I.
  .... Neither do I.

c .... So am I.
  .... So can I.

d .... Oh, I do!
  .... Neither can I.

e .... Oh, I can!
  .... Oh, I don't.

f .... So am I.
  .... Oh, I don't.

6 Job file

1 Look at these pictures.
Which question is the most
suitable for each picture?

Are you good at spelling?
        maths?
        writing letters?
        remembering names?

Can you type fast?
        use a computer?
        write English well?
        speak any foreign languages?

Do you have a driving licence?
        any office skills?
        any sales experience?
        any special qualifications?

Do you like travelling?
        selling things?
        commuting?
        working regular hours?

2 *Group work*

Now take turns asking these questions and
others of your own, like this.

A: Can you type fast, Rosa?
B: Well, not very fast. How about you Sam?
C: Oh, I can't! My typing is terrible! What about you, Kenji?
D: Well, my typing is pretty bad, too.

Useful expressions

Yes.
So-so.
About average.

I suppose so.
Not really.
Actually, no.

3 Now recommend jobs for people in your group.

A: Well, Sam, I think you should be a lifeguard.
B: Yes, you shouldn't be a personal secretary.

INTERCHANGE 10:
NINE TO FIVE

Advertise your skills
and work experience!
Turn to page 135.

7 **Word power:** Adjectives

1 Match these adjectives with definitions.
Then compare with a partner.

a clever   .... has good manners
b easygoing   .... is very intelligent
c forgetful   .... always keeps a promise
d funny   .... thinks deeply about things
e generous   .... doesn't worry about things
f polite   .... likes giving things to people
g reliable   .... doesn't remember things
h serious   .... likes to be around people
i shy   .... likes making people laugh
j sociable   .... doesn't say much in front
                              of other people

2 Can you give definitions for these words?

bad-tempered   creative   patient
prejudiced   talkative

8 **Conversation**

1 Listen.

Myra: Have you met the new sales manager?
John: Yes, I have.
Myra: What do you think of him?
John: Well, he seems OK. He's very serious,
       and he's not very sociable at times.
Myra: Oh, do you think so?
John: Yes, and I think he's a bit forgetful.
       He never remembers my name.
Myra: Yes, you're right. He's very forgetful.
John: Oh, do you know him?
Myra: Yes, he's my husband!
John: Oh … !

2 *Pair work*

Think of three adjectives from the list
in Exercise 7 to describe someone
in the class. Tell them to your partner.
She/He guesses who you are describing.

9 Listening 🔲

1 Listen to four conversations about people. Do you hear something positive (**P**) or negative (**N**)? Circle the correct answer.

a P N   b P N   c P N   d P N

2 Now listen to descriptions of three other people and tick the best adjective to describe each one.

a .... bad-tempered   b .... creative   c .... unfriendly

   .... patient   .... forgetful   .... generous

   .... reliable   .... serious   .... strange

10 Grammar focus: Adjectives and adverbs 🔲

Adjectives	Adverbs and adjectives
He's **serious**.	He's **really serious**.
He's a **serious** man.	He's a **really serious** man.
She's **friendly**.	She's **very friendly**.
She's a **friendly** woman.	She's a **very friendly** woman.
He's not **reliable**.	She's not **very reliable**.
He's not a **reliable** person.	She's not a **very reliable** person.

1 Use the words in brackets to complete the sentences.

a My boss is really .... and he's .... generous.
   (very, easygoing)

b My next door neighbour is not a very .... person. He's a bit ....
   and .... very sociable.
   (not, friendly, shy)

c My sister is .... clever and she's very .... But she's sometimes..................... .
   (creative, really, forgetful)

d My best friend is a .... sociable person, and he's .... too.
   But he's very ....
   (funny, impatient, very)

2 Write a sentence describing yourself. Does your partner agree?

11 Opinion poll

1 **Pair work**

Choose a well-known person to describe. Give as much information as you can.

2 **Class activity**

Now pairs take turns describing the person they talked about. Can anyone guess who it is?

12 Writing

1 Describe two members of your family. How similar or different are they?

My parents are very different. My father is a very serious man. But he's really patient and …

2 *Pair work*

Swap papers and compare your families.

13 Reading: Horoscopes

Read the following horoscopes and write true (**T**) or false (**F**) below, according to the information given.

Let the Stars decide!

Capricorn (Dec 22 – Jan 20) Friends will make you angry this week. Try to understand and be patient.

Aquarius (Jan 21 – Feb 19) Uranus crosses the path of Mars. It means you will have to work harder if you want to be successful.

Pisces (Feb 20 – Mar 20) This is a good time for romance. A stranger will walk into your life, but make sure this person is reliable!

Aries (Mar 21 – Apr 20) Stay in bed this week! You will quarrel with your friends and you will feel depressed and unsociable.

Taurus (Apr 21 – May 21) It is time to do new things. If you want to move house or change job, start making plans now.

Gemini (May 22 – June 21) You will have too much to do, both at home and at work this week. Don't be in a hurry. Friends will help you if you let them.

Cancer (June 22 – Jul 23) Mars entering your star sign will make you very energetic. Be sure to finish whatever you start.

Leo (Jul 24 – Aug 23) There may be one or two small quarrels at home, but they will not be serious. Listen to your family's advice.

Virgo (Aug 24 – Sep 23) This is a good week to make travel plans. Especially if you are going abroad. Be adventurous!

Libra (Sep 24 – Oct 23) You will receive some money, but be very careful. Don't lend it to anybody!

Scorpio (Oct 24 – Nov 22) The full moon will affect your life this week. You could be promoted in your job or win a competition.

Sagittarius (Nov 23 – Dec 21) This week may be pretty busy at work, but your home life will be full of peace and happiness.

a .... This week friends will offer to help people born under the sign of Gemini.

b .... Someone whose birthday is on August 14th was born under the sign of Leo.

c .... People born at the end of October may win something.

d .... Mars will help to give Cancerians a lot of energy this week.

e .... Pisces people will meet someone they don't know this week.

f .... People with the star sign Gemini will not be very busy.

g .... If you are a Leo, you should listen to suggestions from your family this week.

h .... People born under Taurus shouldn't make plans to do anything new.

i .... Sagittarians will have a lot of quarrels at home.

j .... If you were born at the end of March, you will have a good week.

k .... People born at the beginning of January should be patient with their friends.

Unit summary

Grammar

Adverbs of degree

I can type **very** fast.
really fast.
fairly fast.

I can't type **very** fast.

I'm **very** good at languages.
really good at languages.
fairly good at languages.

I'm not **very** good at languages.

Key vocabulary

Nouns
boss
commuting
driving licence
experience
husband
lifeguard
manners
maths
next door neighbour
overtime
personal secretary
phone number
promise
qualification
report
sales manager
salesperson
sales work
skill
spelling
tour guide

Verbs
be good at
enjoy
laugh
meet
worry
write

Modal verbs
can
can't

Adjectives
bad
bad-tempered
clever
creative
easygoing
fast
forgetful
friendly
generous

impatient
intelligent
patient
polite
prejudiced
regular
reliable
serious
shy
sociable
talkative
unfriendly

Adverbs
deeply
well

Other words
neither …
so …

Expressions
Sounds interesting.
So-so.
About average.
I suppose so.
Not really.
Actually, no.

When was it built?

| The passive (simple past, present) | Describing buildings and landmarks |

1 Snapshot

FAMOUS LANDMARKS

The Colosseum in Rome was opened in 80 A.D. It was sometimes filled with water for ship battles.

The Eiffel Tower in Paris was completed in 1889. It was built for the hundredth anniversary of the French Revolution.

The Great Wall of China was begun in 214 B.C. It is the largest structure ever built.

The Taj Mahal in India was built between 1630 and 1652. It is the tomb for the wife of an Indian prince.

The Statue of Liberty in New York was opened in 1886. It was a gift from France to the American people.

Discussion

Do you know anything else about these landmarks?
Have you seen any of them? What are the most famous landmarks in your country?
Are there any famous landmarks where you live?

2 Conversation

1 Listen.

Quizmaster: OK. Quiet, everyone. Let's have two teams for the quiz. Ready?
Bella: Yes.
Mario: Ready.
Quizmaster: Right! Famous canals. Question 1. Who was the Panama Canal built by?
Bella: Well, I think it was started by the French …
Mario: Yes, and it was finished by the Americans!
Quizmaster: OK. One point each! Now, question 2. When was it built?
Bella: 18 …?
Mario: 1920?
Quizmaster: No. It was completed in 1914. No points at all!

2 Now listen to the rest of the conversation.

How long is the canal?
How long does it take to go through it?
How many ships go through it every year?

CARIBBEAN SEA

Panama Canal

COSTA RICA →

PACIFIC OCEAN

PANAMA

COLOMBIA →

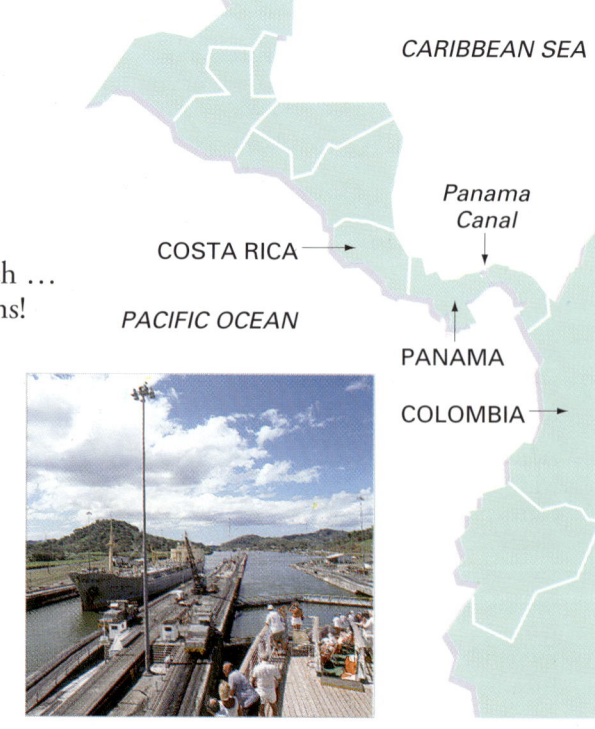

3 **Word power:** Connections

1 The list below contains four kinds of landmarks.
Write the words under the four headings.
Then compare with a partner.

a art gallery   g museum
b bridge   h observatory
c canal   i shrine
d church   j statue
e memorial   k temple
f monument   l tunnel

Things to visit	Religious places	Things connected with transport	Things that commemorate the past

2 **Pair work**

Can you add any more words to each group?

---

4 **Grammar focus:** Past simple passive with *by* 🔲

Active	Passive
The French **started** the Panama Canal.	The Panama Canal **was started by** the French.
The Romans **built** the Colosseum and the Forum.	The Colosseum and the Forum **were built by** the Romans.

1 Complete the phrases in column A with suitable information in column B.
Then compare with a partner.

A

a The novel *1984*
b The pyramids
c The song *Heartbreak Hotel*
d The ceiling of the Sistine chapel in Rome
e The play *Macbeth*

B

.... was sung by Elvis Presley.
.... was written by George Orwell.
.... were built by the ancient Egyptians.
.... was written by Shakespeare.
.... was painted by Michelangelo.

2 Now change these active sentences into passive sentences with *by*. Then compare with a partner.

a Leonardo da Vinci painted the Mona Lisa.
b Marie Curie discovered radium.
c Christiaan Barnard performed the first heart transplant.
d Sir Edmund Hillary and Tenzing Norgay climbed Mount Everest in 1953.
e Thomas Edison invented the light bulb.

5 Pronunciation: Linked sounds

1   Final consonants are often linked to the vowels that follow them.

Paris is one of the most beautiful cities in Europe.

The Colosseum in Rome was opened in 80 A.D.

2   Now mark the linked sounds in these sentences. Listen and check, and then practise them. Pay attention to the linked sounds.

The Museum of Modern Art is a famous art museum in New York.

The Suez Canal in Egypt took many years to build.

Thomas Edison is famous for a lot of inventions.

6 Brain teasers

1   *Pair work*

Think of six questions about famous buildings, landmarks, paintings, books or pieces of music.

Who was *Sunflowers* painted by?
Who was *Madame Bovary* written by?
Who was *Madam Butterfly* composed by?

2   *Group work*

Take turns asking your questions.
Who got the most correct answers?

7 Listening

1   Listen to a tour guide describing some famous buildings in Rome. Take notes and then answer the questions below.

a   When was it finished?
     How many rows of columns were built?
b   When was it built?
     How many storeys does it have?
c   When was it built?
     How many windows were put in?

2   Take turns asking the questions.

a St Peter's

c The Pantheon

b The Colosseum

8 Conversation

Listen.

Linda: Hello, Brook's. Linda speaking. Can I help you?
Mr Abbs: Oh, hello. Yes, I need some information
         about Poland, please.
Linda: Pardon?
Mr Abbs: What currency is used in Poland? Is it the zloty?
Linda: I don't really know. I think so.
Mr Abbs: And do they drive on the right or the left?
Linda: The right, I think, but I'm not sure.
         Listen, what's this …?
Mr Abbs: Just two more things.
         Is much English spoken there?
Linda: I really have no idea.
Mr Abbs: What? Oh well, what about
         credit cards? Are UK Express
         cards accepted?
Linda: How would I know?
Mr Abbs: Well, you *are* a travel agent,
         aren't you?
Linda: A travel agent? This is Brook's
         Hairdressing Salon!
Mr Abbs: Oh, dear! Not Brook's
         Breakaway Holidays?
         Oh, I'm really sorry.
         Wrong number.

9 Grammar focus: Present simple passive without *by*

Active	Passive
They **use** the zloty in Poland.	The zloty **is used** in Poland.
They **speak** both Spanish and Portuguese in Latin America.	Both Spanish and Portuguese **are spoken** in Latin America.

1   Complete these sentences using the passive and one of the verbs below.
      See page 142 for verb lists.

eat   grow   manufacture   speak   teach   wear

a Both cars and computers .... in Korea.

b English .... as a second language in many parts of the USA.

c A lot of cotton .... in Egypt.

d Snails .... in France.

e Kimonos .... sometimes .... in Japan.

f French .... not widely .... in Great Britain.

2   Now use the verbs above and write four sentences like these about your country.
      Use the passive. Then compare with a partner.

10 What do you know?

1 Pair work

How many of these questions can you answer? If you don't know the answers,
look them up on page 142 and make complete sentences for each answer.

a Where is most of the world's coffee grown?
b What languages are spoken in Belgium?
c Where is most of the world's rubber produced?
d Can you name four countries where French is spoken?
e Can you name three countries that are governed by a Prime Minister?

2 Now write down three more world-knowledge questions like these.
Then ask them around the class.

11 Listening

1 Listen to this interview with a Turkish woman.

Where is Turkey situated?
Which countries border Turkey?
How big is it?
What is the population?

2 Now listen to the rest of the interview and fill in the chart.

Capital city: ....

Average income: ....

Religions: ....

Languages: ....

Industries: ....

....

Main exports: ....

....

INTERCHANGE 11:
CULTURE QUIZ

What instrument did
Liberace play? Who
was the song
Material Girl sung by?
Group A turn to page
136 and Group B
to page 138.

12 Reading: The Czech Republic

1   How much do you know about the Czech Republic? Circle the answers below.

   a   Which four of these countries are neighbours to the Czech Republic?
       (Germany, Poland, Hungary, Austria, the Slovak Republic)

   b   The Slovak Republic became formally independent of the Czech Republic in
       (1989, 1991, 1993).

   c   The population of the Czech Republic is a little less than (5 500 000, 10 500 000, 15 500 000).

   d   Brno is the capital of which region? (Bohemia, Moravia)

2   Now read this information. Then check your answers by underlining the correct
      information in the passage.

The Old and the New

The Czech Republic is a mixture of traditional mystery and romance, and new economic and political ideas which modernised the country in the 80s. The country is situated in the middle of Europe and is surrounded by Germany, Austria, Poland and the Slovak Republic, which became a separate state on January 1st 1993.

There are two main areas in the Czech Republic – Bohemia in the west and Moravia in the east. In Moravia you find wooded highlands, castles and vineyards. Brno is the main town of this region. Bohemia, in the west, is hilly and picturesque, with the Krkonose, or Giant Mountains and fairy tale castles, with romantic valleys and lakes, famous spa towns, and its main town Prague, capital of the Republic.

Prague is a truly magnificent city with a population of just over a million – about one tenth of the total population of the country. It has beautiful buildings, excellent hotels and plenty for the visitor to do. There is theatre and opera, a music festival every spring, and plenty of nightlife with clubs and discos for the nightbirds. The Czechs love sports, so football, volleyball, tennis, ice hockey and skiing are all popular. For the less energetic, just walking is very rewarding exercise.

Traditional skills such as fishing, mining, agriculture and forestry continue to form an important part of the Czech economy. Other important areas of production are aircraft, cars, electronics, textiles, leather and glass.

And so the Czech Republic has something to offer everybody from tourist to businessperson. Go and see for yourself!

13 Writing

1   Write a short composition about a country. Include information about situation,
      population and other topics, as above.

2   *Pair work*

      Swap compositions and answer any questions.

Unit summary

Grammar

1   Prepositions with time phrases

> **Years**
> in 1911
> in the 1960s
> during the eighties
>
> **Events**
> before World War I
> during World War II
> after the French Revolution
>
> **Centuries**
> in the fifteenth century
> during the twentieth century

2   Determiners

> A lot of …
> A great deal of …
> Lots of …
> A large amount of …
> A considerable amount of …
> Not much …
> Not very much …
> Very little …
> Hardly any …
> No …

3   For past tense of irregular verbs, see page 142.

Key vocabulary

Nouns
art gallery
bridge
canal
capital
church
cotton
currency
income
industry
information
landmark
light bulb
memorial
monument
museum
novel
observatory
population
rubber
shrine
song
statue
team
temple
travel agent
tunnel
quiz

Verbs
commemorate
complete
compose
discover
drive
govern
grow
manufacture
paint
perform
produce
teach

Adjectives
ancient
right
romantic

Adverb
widely

Preposition
through

Other word
both

Expressions
I'm not sure.
I really have no idea.
How would I know?
Is much English spoken there?
Wrong number.
Oh, dear!

What have you been doing?

> Past simple revision
> Past continuous
> Present perfect continuous
> Adverbial clauses and phrases

1 Conversation

1 Listen.

Jill: Hello! It's Eric Talbot, isn't it?
Eric: Yes, that's right.
Jill: I'm Jill Green. I haven't seen you since we left university!
Eric: Oh, yes! Of course – I remember you! What have you been doing?
Jill: Well, after we graduated I got married, but it didn't work out. So now I'm back at college. How about you?

2 Listen to the rest of the conversation. What did Eric do after graduating?

2 Word power: Verbs and nouns

1 Complete this table. Use a dictionary to help you, if necessary.

Verbs	Nouns
get engaged	....
....	graduation
marry	....
propose	....
....	retirement
separate	....

2 Now use four of the words above to make sentences.

I don't believe in long engagements.

3 Grammar focus: Past simple, past continuous and present perfect continuous

Past simple	Past continuous	Present perfect continuous
I **left** school three years ago. I **got** married in January.	I **was studying** in Britain from 1988–89. I **was living** with my parents before that.	I **have been working** since 1989. We **have been living** in London for two years.

Complete these sentences using a suitable tense and the verbs given. Then compare with a partner.

a Two years ago my sister .... (move) to Australia.

b She .... (work) there when she .... (meet) her husband.

c This time last year I .... (work) in a bank.

d At that time I .... (earn) a lot of money.

e I .... (study) English here for the past six months.

f My family .... (live) in the same house for ten years now.

g I .... (go) to primary school in Edinburgh and secondary school in London.

h I .... (jog) every day for over a year.

4 Listening

Listen to people talking at a party and choose the correct response.

a .... For a year.
   .... A year ago.

b .... Yes, I was.
   .... Yes, I have.

c .... For ten years.
   .... In ten years.

d .... For two years.
   .... In 1990.

e .... Five years ago.
   .... For five years.

f .... In 1987.
   .... Since 1987.

5 Really? How interesting!

1 Pair work

How similar are your experiences to your partner's?
Take turns asking some of these questions and
others of your own.

Did you go to school here?
Did you grow up here?

When did you move here?
Where did you study English before you came here?

What were you doing this time last year?
How about last night at midnight?
And before you started this course?

Have you been studying English long?
Are you studying any other languages, too?
How long have you been talking to me?

Useful expressions

How about you?   How interesting!
Me, too.   Oh, really?
I'm sorry to hear that.

2 Class activity

Tell the class the most interesting thing you learnt about your partner.

6 Snapshot

BEFORE AND AFTER

Jobs some celebrities
once did

Clint Eastwood:
garage attendant

Whoopi Goldberg:
school teacher

Rod Stewart:
grave digger

Arnold Schwarzenegger:
manager of a body building club

Sean Connery:
naval officer

Original names
of some celebrities

Norma Jean Baker
(Marilyn Monroe)

Reginald Dwight
(Elton John)

Maurice Micklethwaite
(Michael Caine)

Annie Mae Bullock
(Tina Turner)

Allen Stewart Konigsberg
(Woody Allen)

Discussion

Do you know any other celebrities who had ordinary jobs and names before they became famous?
Why do you think celebrities sometimes change their names?
If you became a celebrity and wanted to change your name, what name would you choose?

7 Conversation

1   Listen.

Rodney: Well, Sharon, I've been wanting to meet you for ages! The little girl who went to Hollywood! Tell me what happened.

Sharon: Well, after finishing drama school I went to Hollywood to try to get an acting job.

Rodney: Really? Oh, how wonderful!

Sharon: Yes, but I didn't get any work. But after two years I finally got a job with Global Studios.

Rodney: So you finally became an actress! Marvellous!

Sharon: No, I'm a canteen assistant at the studio. But while I'm working, I see a lot of stars!

Rodney: Oh, I see.

2   Now listen to the rest of the conversation. What did Rodney do after he finished college?

8 Grammar focus: Adverbial clauses and phrases

Adverbial clauses

Before I worked in Hollywood, I was a student.
After I left school, I went to Hollywood.
While I was living in Hollywood, I tried to get an acting job.
Since I've lived here, I've made a lot of friends.

Adverbial phrases

During the week, I used to study.
Before 1992, I didn't work.
After two years in Hollywood, I finally got a job.

Shortened forms

Before working in Hollywood, …
After leaving school, …
While living in Hollywood, …
Since living here, …

1   Write shortened forms of these adverbial clauses.

a   While I was going to college, I had a part-time job in a TV studio.
b   Before Heidi became a teacher, she worked in a bank.
c   Since he's come to England, Toshi's English has improved a lot.
d   After he graduated from university, Ken was unemployed for six months.
e   Since she's learnt to drive, Mariella has been all over Europe.

2   Complete these clauses and phrases with information about yourself or someone you know. Then compare with a partner.

a   While attending school …
b   During my childhood …
c   Since starting this course …
d   Before I came to school today …
e   Before 1993 …
f   After leaving home today …

9 Pronunciation: Sentence stress

1 Notice the stressed words in these sentences.

When I was a **stud**ent, I studied **dra**ma.
While **stud**ying **dra**ma, I **read** a **lot** of **Shake**speare.
After I **grad**uated, I **tra**velled round **Eur**ope.

2 Now listen and practise the sentences you made in Exercise 8.1.

10 Hidden secrets

Class activity

Go round the class and try to find people who did the following things. Stop after five minutes.
How many names do you have?

Did you …	Names
a have any bad habits when you were young?	....
b drive a car before you passed the test?	....
c use to stay away from school when you weren't ill?	....
d ever try to cheat in exams?	....
e go to clubs when you were under age?	....

11 Listening

1 *Group work*

How much do you know about
these people?

Who are they? Where and when were they born?
What did they do before they became famous?
What are some of the important things
they did during their lives?
How and when did they die?

a

b

c

2 Now listen to information about each person and take notes.

3 *Pair work*

Take turns. Choose one of the people and use your notes to talk about her/his life.

12 Reading

1 Read this passage.

'A Skill and Musicality to Rival Any'

It is 27 July, 1989 in a large concert hall in London. The audience prepares itself for a unique event in the history of classical music. The first solo percussion recital in the 95 years of the famous 'Promenade Concerts'. The performer is Evelyn Glennie, a small colourful figure, not only young and female in a male world – she is also the first full-time British solo percussionist. She has also been profoundly deaf from the age of 12.

Born on a farm in north east Scotland in 1965, Evelyn Glennie had, in her words, a very ordinary childhood, sharing the normal farm work, the fights and the games with her two older brothers, Colin and Roger. She first learnt the piano at an early age, and only began to have problems with hearing when she was eight. 'I wonder if I'm losing my hearing,' she wrote in her diary, but nobody else noticed it at that time. Later, at the age of 12, her hearing was so poor that her parents were advised to send her to a special school. Evelyn, however, refused to go to a school where she would not have her music, and finally went to a normal secondary school. She told nobody about her deafness at first, and was actually considered very unmusical!

As her deafness got worse, her love of music increased and she learnt to feel rhythms through her hands and feet. She managed to win a place at the Royal Academy of Music, in London, where she studied all kinds of percussion instruments. She also appeared on TV, radio and in magazines.

After graduating in 1985, she started her solo career, travelling to Rio de Janeiro, Japan, the USA, Switzerland and Scandinavia, a star of truly international standing.

Her comments on this extraordinary career? 'I'm glad, at last, that people are talking about my music, not my deafness.'

2 *Pair work*

Cover the passage. How many things can you remember about Evelyn Glennie?

3 How do you explain the success of people like Evelyn Glennie?

13 Writing

1 Write a short biography of an interesting person in your family (e.g., a grandparent, aunt or uncle) or of a famous person you like or admire.

My grandmother came to England from Poland when she was thirteen. She couldn't speak any English, so she …

2 *Pair work*

Swap papers and answer any questions your partner may have.

> **INTERCHANGE 12:**
> THE ROVING REPORTER
>
> Would you enjoy reporting on the rich and famous?
> Student A turn to page 137 and Student B to page 139.

Unit summary

Grammar

1   Adverbials of time

> for about six months
> for eighteen months
> for less than a year
> for the last two years
> for ages
> for a long time
> for as long as I can remember
> less than a year ago
> over a year ago
> since my childhood
> since I got married
> since then
> since that time
> this time last year
> the year before last

2   See page 143 for a list of tenses and verb forms.

Key vocabulary

Nouns
acting job
actress
biography
body building club
canteen
celebrity
course
drama
driving test
engagement
grandparent
grave digger
habit
life
naval officer
parent
part
retirement
star
studio

Verbs
cheat
die
get engaged
get married
graduate
improve
propose
separate

Adjectives
ill
ordinary
part-time
same
unemployed

Adverbs
back
finally
over a year

Prepositions
during
since

Expressions
It didn't work out.
I'm sorry to hear that.
How interesting.
Oh, really?
How about you?

Review

1 What about you?

Group work

One student makes a statement about one of the following.

something you … are good at or not good at
can do well or can't do well
like or don't like
hate doing

Then the student points to someone else in the group. That student responds and makes another statement, like this.

A: I hate doing housework. (points to someone)
B: So do I.
I can't sing. (points to someone)
C: I can!

Useful responses

So am I / Neither am I / I am! / I'm not!
So can I / Neither can I / I can! / I can't!
So do I / Neither do I / I do! / I don't!

2 My kind of person

1 Group work

What do you think are the three most important qualities for (a) a friend and (b) a wife or husband? Choose from these adjectives or use adjectives of your own.

clever   funny   hardworking   patient   serious
easygoing   generous   independent   reliable   sociable

Talk about them like this.   I think a friend should be …
It's important for a husband to be …

2 Class activity

Compare your choices.

3 What do you know?

1 Group work

Write five true and five false statements about places, famous buildings or landmarks.

Spanish is spoken in Chile. (T)   Rice is grown in England. (F) (India)

2 Class activity

Take turns. One group reads its statements and another group decides whether they are true or false.

4   Listening

Listen to people on a TV game show
answer questions about Spain.
What are the correct answers?
Take notes.

a   currency   ....

b   driving   ....

c   population   ....

d   capital   ....

e   popular sport   ....

f   neighbouring countries   ....

5   Can you remember?

Pair work

Take turns asking   What were you doing …   How long have you been …
these questions.   four hours ago?   living here?
                         at nine o'clock yesterday?   sitting there?
                         at this time yesterday?   wearing those clothes?

6   Star talk

Group work

One student in the group talks about one of these famous people from the notes below.
The other students in the group close their books and try to guess who it is.

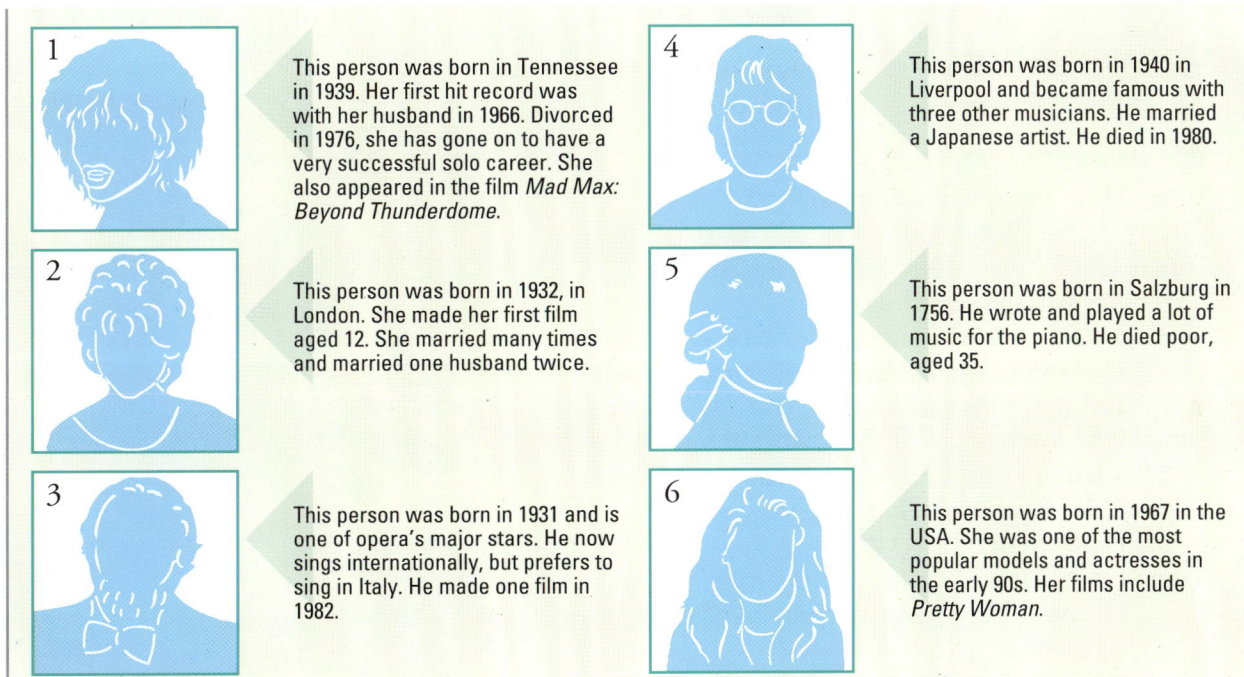

1   This person was born in Tennessee in 1939. Her first hit record was with her husband in 1966. Divorced in 1976, she has gone on to have a very successful solo career. She also appeared in the film *Mad Max: Beyond Thunderdome*.

4   This person was born in 1940 in Liverpool and became famous with three other musicians. He married a Japanese artist. He died in 1980.

2   This person was born in 1932, in London. She made her first film aged 12. She married many times and married one husband twice.

5   This person was born in Salzburg in 1756. He wrote and played a lot of music for the piano. He died poor, aged 35.

3   This person was born in 1931 and is one of opera's major stars. He now sings internationally, but prefers to sing in Italy. He made one film in 1982.

6   This person was born in 1967 in the USA. She was one of the most popular models and actresses in the early 90s. Her films include *Pretty Woman*.

Answers on page 142.

What's on?

Past and present participles	*bored, boring*
Relative clauses	*the person who …*
Talking about films and books	*the thing that …*

1 Snapshot

TEN TOP FILMS

Ten of the world's most successful films since 1975

Jaws (1975)
Return of the Jedi (1983)
Star Wars (1977)
Raiders of the Lost Ark (1981)
The Empire Strikes Back (1980)
Batman (1989)
Indiana Jones and the Temple of Doom (1984)
Ghost (1992)
ET (1982)
Jurassic Park (1993)

Discussion

How many of these films have you seen? Which one is your favourite / your least favourite?
What are the three best films you have seen in the last year?
What kinds of films do you like best?

2 Conversation 📼

1 Listen.

Alma: How about a film tonight?
Kate: Maybe. What's on?
Alma: There's a new Dirty Harry film on.
Are you interested?
Kate: Oh, no! I can't stand Clint Eastwood!
He's so boring. All he does is stand around
and try to look macho!
Alma: Oh, come on! Well then, what about
a James Dean film? They're showing
Rebel Without a Cause at Cinema City.
Fancy that?
Kate: Now that sounds more interesting!
I've never seen it, and I really like James Dean.

2 Now listen to the rest of the conversation.
What happened next? What did they decide to do?

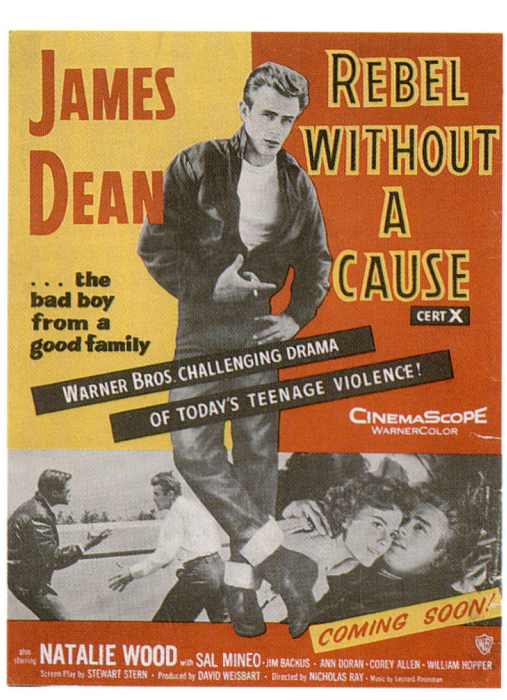

3 Grammar focus: Participles 🔲

Past participles	Present participles
I'm **interested** in old films.	Old films are **interesting**.
I was **bored** by the book.	The book was **boring**.
I was **surprised** by the film's ending.	The film's ending was **surprising**.

1 Complete these sentences with the past or present participle of the words in brackets.

   a I'm not .... in horror films. (interest)

   b I find nature films .... (fascinate)

   c I'm .... with watching television. (bore)

   d I didn't like *Batman* at all. I'm .... that it was so successful. (surprise)

   e *Star Wars* was a really .... film. (excite)

   f Meryl Streep is a very .... actress. (interest)

   g I'm .... by Stephen King's novels. (fascinate)

   h I thought *The Russia House* was a .... book. (bore)

   i It's .... they don't make many westerns these days. (surprise)

2 Now write six sentences like the ones above about films, actors, actresses or novels. Use your own information. Then compare with a partner. Does your partner agree?

4 Let's go to the cinema!

1 *Pair work*

   Take turns asking these questions and others of your own.

   How often do you go to the cinema?
   What kinds of films are you interested in?
   What kinds of films don't you like? Why?
   Do you have a favourite actor?
   Who's your favourite actress?
   What's one of the best films you have ever seen?
   What did you like about it?
   What are your three favourite films in English?
   Are there any interesting films on now?

2 *Group work*

   Compare your information.

5 Pronunciation: Word stress

1 Mark the stress in these words on the first or second syllable. Listen and check, and then practise them.

favourite   ridiculous   surprising   terrific
interesting   successful   terrible   unusual

2 Now listen and practise these sentences.

Jurassic Park is my favourite film. I thought *Ghostbusters 2* was ridiculous.
Robert de Niro is a terrific actor.

6 Word power: Adjectives

1 *Pair work*

Add these words to
the word map.

boring
disgusting
fascinating
odd
pointless
ridiculous
silly
terrible
terrific
unusual
weird
wonderful

awful

stupid

Reactions

exciting

strange

2 Now look at these words. Do they describe a positive (+) or a negative (–) reaction?

dreadful ......   fantastic ......   marvellous ......   pathetic ......
excellent ......   horrible ......   outstanding ......   superb ......

3 *Pair work*

Use some of the adjectives above to describe the most recent film you've seen.
Pay attention to word stress.

7 Listening

Listen to some people talking about books and films. Tick the best adjective to describe what they think about each one.

a .... fascinating   .... silly   .... strange
b .... wonderful   .... odd   .... boring
c .... boring   .... terrific   .... dreadful
d .... ridiculous   .... interesting .... exciting

8 Conversation

Listen.

Paul: Oh, *Jane Eyre*. I've never read it. Isn't it boring? What's it like?
Rene: Well, it's a book that we're reading at school.
Paul: It must be boring, then! What's it about?
Rene: It's about a woman who works as a governess in a large house …
Paul: Fascinating!
Rene: … and she falls in love with her employer …
Paul: It still doesn't sound very exciting.
Rene: … but he's already married to a horrible mad woman who lives upstairs locked away in a room.
Paul: That sounds more interesting! Can I borrow it?

9 Grammar focus: Relative clauses

> Use *who* or *that* for people.
>
> It's about a woman. She falls in love with her employer.
> It's about a woman **who/that** falls in love with her employer.
>
> There are many people. They enjoy reading.
> There are many people **who/that** enjoy reading.
>
> Use *which* or *that* for things.
>
> It's a book. We're reading it at school.
> It's a book **which/that** we're reading at school.
>
> There are many stories. They don't sound very interesting.
> There are many stories **which/that** don't sound very interesting.

1 Join these sentences with *who, that* or *which*. Then compare with a partner.

a *West Side Story* is a musical. It was composed in the fifties.
b Leonard Bernstein was a composer. He wrote the music for *West Side Story*.
c There are many famous American actors. They have made a lot of good films.
d *War and Peace* is a book. It is really fascinating.
e *Cyrano de Bergerac* is a play. It was made into a film.
f The film *Thelma and Louise* is about two women. They travel across America.
g Steven Spielberg is a director. He has made many successful films.
h *ET* is a science fiction film. It has made over £130 million.

2 *Pair work*

Complete these sentences with relative clauses.

a Sean Connery is an actor …
b *Jurassic Park* is a film …
c Marilyn Monroe was an actress …
d Walt Disney was a famous film director …
e *Batman* is a film …
f Mia Farrow is an actress …
g Gerard Depardieu is an actor …

10 Script writers

1   Group work

You are script writers for a television studio. You have to write a new script for a TV detective series. Think of a good story, and discuss these questions.

Where does the story take place?
Who are the main characters?
What happens?
How does the story end?

2   Class activity

Now tell the class about your story.

Our story is about a bank robbery that takes place in Chicago. There are three main characters ...

Decide which story would be best for television.

11   Listening

1   Listen to two critics discussing a new film on *A Night at the Films*. What do they like or not like about it? Mark the chart like this:

3 = liked it very much
2 = OK
1 = didn't like it

	Pauline	Colin
Acting	....	....
Story	....	....
Photography	....	....
Special effects	....	....

2   First guess how many stars each critic gave the film.

★★★★ excellent   ★★★ good   ★★ fair   ★ poor

Pauline ....
Colin   ....

3   Now listen to the critics give their ratings.

Pauline ....
Colin   ....

INTERCHANGE 13:
FILM TRIVIA

Are you mad about films?
Turn to page 140.

12 Reading: Film reviews

1   Read these film critics' reviews of
    The Last Emperor. How do you think
    each critic rated the film?

Film Director's Last Epic

In The Last Emperor, director Bernardo
Bertolucci not only gives us a fascinating
history lesson but also a compelling human
drama. It is the story of Pu Yi, who came to the
throne in 1908 at the age of 2. The
performances are outstanding, and the film is
spectacular in every way. The 3 hours fly by,
and the audience leaves feeling they have got to
know a great country and a sensitive, unusual
man.

The Reviewer

Critic's rating ....

What a drag!

Bernardo Bertolucci is a talented
director. Why he made The Last
Emperor is a mystery. True, the
scenery and costumes are nice. But
the main character is passive and dull
– he simply watches his life go by.
You'd expect a film which covers 60
years of history to be exciting. But the
3 hours of The Last Emperor drag on
forever. At least the film is consistent
– consistently boring.

The Standard

Critic's rating ....

The Emperor's New Clothes

Don't go and see The Last Emperor if you're expecting a history
lesson. Bertolucci's epic about the rise and fall of Pu Yi is hard to
follow and confusing at times. But he has done a remarkable job of
portraying the Chinese culture, and has captured China in stunningly
beautiful images. There are some touching scenes, as when the
young Pu Yi's nurse is taken from him. Unfortunately, the film is
too long and tends to drag at times.

The Gazette

Critic's rating ....

2   Pair work

Which words in each review helped you decide on the critics' ratings?

13 Writing

1   Pair work

Choose a film you have both seen recently and discuss it. Then write a review of it
using these questions as a guide.

What was the film about?   What did you like or not like about it?
Did you enjoy it?   How would you rate it?

2   Class activity

Now swap reviews. Do you agree?

Unit summary

Grammar

Verbs with prepositions

> I am amazed **at/by** …
> I was bored **by/with** …
> He is excited **at/by** …
>   fascinated **by** …
>   interested **in** …
>   pleased **at/with** …
>   surprised **at/by** …
>   worried **by** …

Key vocabulary

Nouns
actor
character
composer
critic
detective
director
employer
event
governess
horror film
million
music
musical
nature film
reaction
review
robbery
science fiction
script
story
western

Verbs
end
fancy
kill
lock
rate
stand around
take place

Adjectives
best
better
boring
disgusting
dreadful
excellent
fantastic
fair
fascinating
horrible
macho
main
marvellous

negative
odd
outstanding
pathetic
pointless
poor
positive
ridiculous
silly
strange
stupid
successful
superb
surprising
unusual
weird
wonderful

Relative pronouns
that
which
who

Other words
all
not … at all

Expressions
What's on?
What's it about?
What's it like?
How about …?
I can't stand …
Oh, come on!

Look before you leap!

Modals and adverbs	*must, have to, may, might, can, could, probably, perhaps, maybe*
Reported speech Making excuses	

1 Snapshot

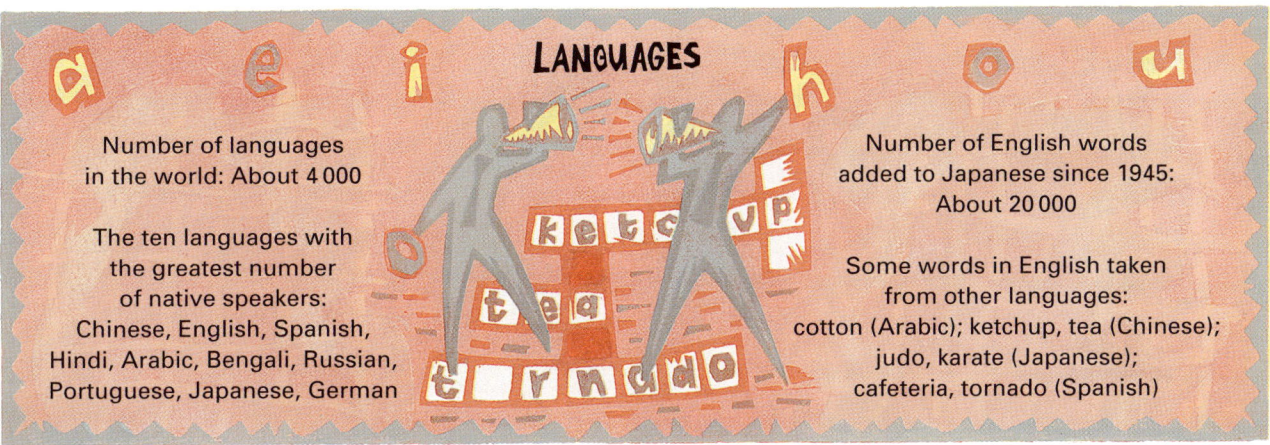

Number of languages in the world: About 4 000

The ten languages with the greatest number of native speakers: Chinese, English, Spanish, Hindi, Arabic, Bengali, Russian, Portuguese, Japanese, German

LANGUAGES

Number of English words added to Japanese since 1945: About 20 000

Some words in English taken from other languages: cotton (Arabic); ketchup, tea (Chinese); judo, karate (Japanese); cafeteria, tornado (Spanish)

Discussion

Can you name some countries where these languages are spoken: Arabic, Portuguese and Spanish? Think of ten common words in your language that come from other languages.

2 Conversation

1   Listen.

Ken: I'm glad we hired this car for our holiday. Now we can really get around and see the sights.

Sammy: Yes. You know these main roads are fantastic, but the road signs can be a bit confusing.

Ken: What do these lines on the road mean?

Sammy: They may mean you can't overtake here.

Ken: Well, I'm going to, anyway. I want to get past this car. It's going much too slowly. Now, I wonder what this sign means.

Sammy: I think it means you have to turn left if you're in this lane.

Ken: Yes, perhaps, but perhaps it means that you can turn left if you want to. I think I'll just go straight on.

2   Now listen to the rest of the conversation. Which picture shows the road they were driving on? Which sign is the police officer talking about?

3 Grammar focus: Modals and adverbs 🔲

> This sign **may** mean you **can** overtake here.
> That **might** mean you **have to** turn right.
> It **could** mean you **must** turn left there.
>
> It **probably** means there's no overtaking.
> **Perhaps** it means you **can't** overtake here.
> **Maybe** that means you **can** do a U-turn.

1   What do you think these signs mean? Make sentences as in the grammar box, choosing suitable phrases from those below. Then compare with a partner.

Perhaps (a) means ...

- there's a steep hill ahead.
- there's a level crossing ahead.
- this area is reserved for wheelchairs.
- you should give way to traffic at the next junction.
- there's a pedestrian crossing ahead.
- the road is slippery when it's wet.
- there are roadworks ahead.
- you should look out for falling rocks.
- you can't do a U-turn here.

2   *Pair work*

Now talk about these signs. What do you think they could mean?

4 **Word power:** Definitions

1 Match each word with a definition. Then compare with a partner.

A: What does … mean?
B: It means …

a proverb (n)   .... tell
b articulate (adj)   .... change something from one language into another
c talkative (adj)   .... someone who does not tell the truth
d translate (v)   .... stop someone talking by starting to talk
e interrupt (v)   .... group of words that are very difficult to say
f relate (v)   .... very good at speaking
g liar (n)   .... talking a lot
h tongue-twister (n)   .... a saying people use

2 *Pair work*

Can you give definitions for these words? Use a dictionary to help you, if necessary.

apologise (v)   criticise (v)   idiom (n)   fluent (adj)   dialect (n)   slang (n)

5 **Proverbs**

1 *Group work*

Here are some common proverbs in English. What do you think they mean?

Don't count your chickens before they're hatched.
A stitch in time saves nine.
Don't burn your bridges.
Every cloud has a silver lining.
One person's meat is another one's poison.
Look before you leap.
An eye for an eye, a tooth for a tooth.

Talk about them like this:

I think it means …   Well, it could mean …
Or perhaps it means …   It probably means …

2 Now think of some interesting proverbs in your own language and write them down in English. What do they mean? Discuss with a partner.

3 *Class activity*

Tell the class about one of the proverbs you discussed.

6 Listening

1 Listen to Albert inviting friends to his birthday party.
What excuses do people make for not coming?
Draw a line from each person to the excuse she/he makes.

Scott   She said that she wasn't feeling well.
     He said he was taking his mother dancing.
Yoko   She said she had guests for the weekend.
Manuel   He said that he would be away.
     She said she was going out with a friend.
Regina   He said he was going away with his family.

2 Now it's the night of Albert's birthday party. Listen. What happened?

7 Grammar focus: Reported speech

Statement	Reported speech
I **am** not **feeling** well.	She said (that) she **was** not **feeling** well.
I **am taking** my mother out.	He said he **was taking** his mother out.
I **have made** other plans.	She said she **had made** other plans.
I **didn't get** the invitation.	He said he **hadn't got** the invitation.
I **will be** away.	She said she **would be** away.
I **can't come**.	She said she **couldn't come**.
I **may go** ice skating.	She said she **might go** ice skating.
There **is** an office party.	He said there **was** an office party.

Look at these excuses. Change them into reported speech and then compare with a partner.

Susie: 'I have to visit my grandparents.'

Susie said she had to visit her grandparents.

a Bob: 'I am going away for the weekend.'
b Mary: 'I have been invited to a wedding on Saturday.'
c Jim: 'I promised to help Joanne move.'
d Ann: 'I can't come because I've got flu.'
e John: 'I will be studying for a test all weekend.'
f Sharon: 'I have to meet someone at the airport.'

8 Never on Sunday!

1 Your teacher wants to have an extra class on Sunday afternoon. You don't want to go. Make up an excuse.

I'm taking my dog to the hairdresser.

2 *Class activity*

Tell your partner your excuse. Your partner then reports your excuse to the class.

She said she was taking her dog to the hairdresser.

3 Which was the best excuse you heard? Tell the class.

9 Listening and writing

Nancy is away for the weekend.
Listen to four messages on her answering
machine. Her flatmate has written
down the first one. Write down the
other three messages.

> **WHILE YOU WERE OUT**
>
> Date *Friday* Time *9 p.m.*
> Message *Bill called. He
> said he would meet you in
> front of Pizza House at
> 6.30 p.m. on Monday.*

10 Pronunciation: Information focus

1 If we want to emphasise one piece of information in a sentence we give it extra stress.
Listen to these examples.

A: John said he'd meet you at the library on **Friday**.
B: Oh, I thought he said **Thursday**.

A: John said he'd meet you at the **library** on Friday.
B: Oh, I thought he said at the **station**.

2 Now listen to this sentence spoken in three different ways.
Underline the stressed word in each case.

a Terry said he was going to a football match on Friday.
b Terry said he was going to a football match on Friday.
c Terry said he was going to a football match on Friday.

3 Can you match the appropriate questions to each of the sentences?

1 **When** is Terry going?
2 **Who** is going to the football match?
3 **Where** is Terry going?

4 *Pair work*

Make up three sentences about your own plans and read them to your partner.
She/He will ask you to repeat your sentence with a different stress pattern.

A: I'm going to see my brother at the weekend.
B: **Who** are you going to see?
A: I'm going to see my **brother**.

113

11 Reading: The truth about lying

Do you ever make excuses that are not really true? When and why?
It seems that everybody tells lies – well, not big lies, but what we call 'white lies'. These are usually lies to protect other people – or ourselves. A recent study found that in conversation people frequently stretch the truth. Here are some ways they do it.

1 **Lying to hide something:** People often lie because they want to hide something from someone. For example, a son doesn't tell his parents that he is going out with a girl because he doesn't think they will like her. Instead he says he's going out with some friends.

2 **Making up untrue excuses:** Sometimes people lie because they don't want to do something. For example, someone invites you to a party. You think it will be boring so you say that you have something else planned.

3 **Lying to make someone feel good:** Often we stretch the truth to make someone feel good. For example, your friend cooks dinner for you, but it tastes terrible. Do you say so? No! You probably say 'Mmm, this is delicious!'

4 **Lying to hide bad news:** Sometimes we don't want to tell someone bad news. For example, you have just had a very bad argument with your boy/girlfriend, but you don't want to talk about it. So if someone asks how things are between you, you just say everything is fine.

'No, nothing's the matter. Everything's fine, I tell you.'

Telling white lies isn't really bad. Most of the time people do it because they want to protect a friendship.

1   Do you know any other reasons people tell white lies?

2   *Pair work*

Now look at these situations. Are they examples of 1, 2, 3, or 4?
More than one answer is possible.

a You borrowed a friend's motorbike and scratched it. You are having it painted. The friend wants the motorbike back. You say the engine didn't sound right and you are having it checked.
b Your friend gives you an ugly vase for your birthday. You say 'Oh! It's beautiful!'
c Someone you don't like invites you to a film, so you say 'I've already seen it.'
d You're planning a surprise party for a friend. To get her to come to your house at the right time, you ask her to come round and see your new video player.

INTERCHANGE 14:
WHO SAID THAT?

What do other people in the class think about things? Turn to page 140 for some searching questions.

Unit summary

Key vocabulary

Nouns
bridge
cloud
conversation
dialect
excuse
falling rock
flatmate
flu
guest
hairdresser
hill
ice skating
idiom
invitation
judo
junction
karate
ketchup
lane
lesson
liar
library
line
lining
parking space
pedestrian crossing
plan
poison
proverb
road works
road sign
saying
silver
slang
stitch
tongue-twister
tooth
tornado
traffic
truth
U-turn
wheelchair

Verbs
apologise
burn
count
criticise
feel
get around
give way
hire
interrupt
leap
look out
overtake
promise
relate
translate
wonder

Modal verbs
can
could
have to
may
might
must
should

Adjectives
articulate
confusing
disabled
fluent
glad
reserved
slippery
steep
talkative
wet

Adverbs
ahead
anyway
perhaps
slowly
straight on

Other words
another
every

Expression
We can see the sights.

Decisions! Decisions!

Second conditional	Modals: *could, should, might*
Third conditional	Past modals: *could have, should have, might have*
	Talking about hypothetical situations and problems

1 Snapshot

BREAKING THE RECORD

The highest price paid for an autograph: £200 000 for a letter signed by Thomas Jefferson sold in 1986.

The largest discovery of treasure: £670 million from a Russian ship sunk in 1905.

The most valuable archaeological treasure: King Tutankhamen's tomb, Egypt 1922.

The biggest fine: In 1986 Ivan Boesky was fined £65 000 000 for insider trading.

The biggest loss of jewellery: Jewellery worth £12 000 000 disappeared from a villa in Cannes in the south of France on July 24th 1980.

Discussion

Have you ever won anything? Have you ever lost or found anything valuable?

2 Conversation

Listen.

Howard: Look at this! Someone who worked for 30 years as a bank clerk has inherited five million pounds!

Janice: Really?

Howard: Yes, from some relative of his he'd never even met. Why don't I have any relatives like that?

Janice: Well, what would you do if you inherited five million?

Howard: Oh, decisions, decisions! Well, I think I'd give some of it to charity, to start with. Then I'd give up my job in the bank and buy a boat and sail round the world. What about you?

Janice: I wouldn't do that. I'd buy all the empty houses in London, repair and decorate them and then sell them really cheaply to people who need them.

Howard: I think you'd need more than five million!

3 Grammar focus: Second conditional sentences and modals

> What **would** you do **if you had £5 million?**
> **If I had £5 million**, I **would** sail around the world.
> I **might** give up my job.
> **I'd** probably give some money to charity.
> I **wouldn't** spend it all at once.

1 Complete the clauses in column A with suitable information in column B.
There may be more than one possibility for each one. Then compare with a partner.

A

a If I found a burglar in my house,
b If I saw someone shoplifting,
c If I found a lot of money,
d If my hotel room was very cold,
e If I locked myself out of my house,
f If I didn't like the meal I was served
   in a restaurant,

B

.... I'd break a window to get in.
.... I'd run to my neighbours for help.
.... I might not tell anybody.
.... I'd probably call the police.
.... I think I might spend it.
.... I wouldn't pay for it.
.... I might tell a sales assistant.
.... I'd complain to the manager.

2 Now complete the clauses in column A with your own ideas. Then compare with a partner.

3 *Pair work*

Now think of three more situations like the ones above. Then ask another pair of
students what they would do.

4 Predicaments

1 *Group work*

What would you do in the situations below?

A: What would you do if …?
B: I think I'd …
C: I'm not sure, but I might …

– you found a valuable piece of
  jewellery on a park bench.
– a friend borrowed some money
  from you and didn't return it.
– you were on holiday abroad and
  lost all your money and credit cards.
– you saw two people fighting in the street.
– you discovered your friend had stolen
  something from a shop.

2 *Class activity*

Choose three of the best suggestions and
tell the class about them.

5 Listening

1 Listen to these three people talking about three different predicaments. What are they?
Write them in the chart below.

2 Now listen again. What do you think the best suggestion was for each predicament?
Complete the chart and compare answers around the class.

	Predicament	Best suggestion
a	....	....
b	....	....
c	....	....

6 Word power: Verbs

1 Find nine pairs of opposites in this list. Then compare with a partner.

accept	borrow	dislike	find	lose	remember
admit	deny	divorce	forget	marry	save
agree	disagree	enjoy	lend	refuse	spend

2 *Pair work*

Now choose four pairs of opposites
and use each pair in a sentence.

I can never save money because I spend it all on clothes.

7 Conversation

1 Listen.

Paula: Hi, Wendy! You look tired!
Is your visitor still staying with you?
Wendy: She's just gone, finally, after three weeks.
Thank goodness!
Paula: So how did you get her to go in the end?
Wendy: Well, I told her a white lie and
said my parents were coming at the
weekend and I needed the room.
I feel bad about it, though.
What would you have done?
Paula: Oh, I would have told her to leave
after a week! By the way, my
father-in-law is coming to
stay with us next week. Can I move
in with you for a few days?
Wendy: Certainly not!

2 If this happened to you, what would you do?

8 Pronunciation: Weak form of *have* 🔲

1   Listen to the weak form of *have* in these sentences.

What would you have done?   What would you have said?
          /juəv/   /juəv/

I would have told her to leave.   I wouldn't have said anything.
   /aɪdəv/   /aɪwədn̩təv/

2   Now practise these sentences. Use the weak form of *have*.

You could have said something.
You should have told me.
You might have asked me about it.
You shouldn't have said anything.

9 Grammar focus: Third conditional sentences and past modals 🔲

What **would** you **have done**?	I **would have told** her to leave. I **wouldn't have done** anything. I **would have asked** her about it.
What **should** I **have done**?	You **could have spoken** to her about it. You **shouldn't have made** her leave.

1   Read the situations in column A. What do you think would have been the best thing to do?
Choose suitable suggestions from column B and then compare with a partner.
There may be more than one possibility for each one.

A
a My aunt gave me a cigarette lighter for my birthday. But I don't smoke.
b I saw a colleague stealing some money from work. So I wrote her a letter about it.
c A friend of mine is always late. So I bought him an alarm clock.
d I hit someone's car as I was leaving a parking space. Luckily no one saw me.
e A friend borrowed my favourite book and spilled coffee all over it.

B
.... You should have spoken to him about it.
.... I would have told her that I'd prefer something else.
.... I would have spoken to the friend about it.
.... I would have waited for the owner to come back.
.... You could have changed it for something else.
.... I wouldn't have said anything.
.... You could have warned her not to do it again.
.... You could have left a note for the owner.

2   *Pair work*

Now give another suggestion for each situation. Use the weak form of *have*.
Then compare answers round the class.

10 Second chances

1   Think about things that have happened in your life during the last few years.
    What opportunities did you miss? Write down five things you should or shouldn't
    have done, like this.

> I should have married my first girlfriend.
> I shouldn't have left my job.

2   *Group work*

    Now talk about your missed opportunities.

11 Listening

1   Listen to three people phoning Dr Hill, a counsellor on a radio talk show.
    Make notes in the chart below.

	What was the problem?	What did they do?	What should they have done?
1st caller	....	....	....
2nd caller	....	....	....
3rd caller	....	....	....

INTERCHANGE 15:
WHAT WOULD YOU
HAVE DONE?

Sometimes there are
no right answers! Turn
to page 141 and see
what you would have
done in these difficult
situations.

2   Do you agree with Dr Hill?
    What advice would you have given?

12 Reading: Kate Manners

Read these letters to Kate Manners' advice column and find the most suitable reply to each one.

1

Dear Kate

I am a young widow with two small children, aged 1 and 3. I used to live with my mum who loves the children, but who kept interfering in everything I did. Since I've moved out, I'm terribly lonely and depressed as I can never go out and have no adults to talk to.

Lonely

2

Dear Kate

I recently heard a silly rumour about a colleague of mine at work. I'm afraid I told several people about it, and my colleague found out about it as well. But now I find the rumour simply isn't true. What should I do?

Worried

3

Dear Kate

My daughter's new boyfriend came to dinner with us last week. Frankly, he was awful – dressed in old jeans, with a pony tail and earrings. My husband and I didn't say much to him, and weren't particularly friendly as we were rather shocked. My daughter won't talk to us now and has threatened to move out. She's only just eighteen.

A Mother

c

Dear ▢

In your situation I think you need all the help you can get, and if I were you, I would stay at your mother's for a couple more years. Having another adult around helps beat that loneliness, and will also give you a chance to get out now and then.

Kate

a

Dear ▢

I think you should have been a little more tolerant and made your daughter's friend more welcome. He's probably got some good qualities, and after all, your daughter doesn't have to live with you. You will lose her if you are rude to her friends.

Kate

b

Dear ▢

Well, you've learnt a lesson. You shouldn't have listened to gossip. Now you have to repair the damage. The best thing is to tell your friends the story you told them isn't true. You should also apologise sincerely to your colleague and hope that they will forgive and forget.

Kate

d

Dear ▢

You should have thought more carefully before you acted as you did. It really wasn't necessary to get angry. The best thing to do in situations like that is to speak to the person immediately and warn him or her not to do it again.

Kate

13 Writing

1 Pair work

Write a letter to Kate Manners about a problem situation like the ones in Exercise 12.

2 Class activity

Put your letters on the board. Then choose a letter and reply to it.

Unit summary

Key vocabulary

Nouns
alarm clock
aunt
boat
burglar
cigarette lighter
colleague
competition
discovery
father-in-law
fine
jewellery
neighbour
note
owner
park bench
police
price
relative
sales assistant
visitor
window

Verbs
accept
admit
agree
bite
borrow
break
change
decorate
deny
disagree
discover
dislike
fight
give up
inherit
interfere
lend
lose
prefer
refuse
repair
sail
shoplift
steal
warn
white lie

Adjectives
empty
tired
valuable

Adverbs
abroad
cheaply
luckily

Other words
all at once
no one
piece of
someone
something else
though

Expressions
Thank goodness!
Certainly not!

Review

1 Critics' choice

1 Group work

What are the three best films you have seen recently?

Why do you think these three films are the best? Talk about the subjects below and then rank the most popular films from 1 to 3 (1 = best).

the story	the photography	the scenery
the acting	the music	why you liked it so much

2 Class activity

Now report on your favourite film to the class.

2 Spare time

1 Group work

What are your favourite spare time activities?
Ask these questions and talk about what you do in your free time.

How many hours do you watch TV every day?
What kinds of TV programmes do you like?
What do you think are the most interesting programmes at the moment?

Are you interested in sport?
How often do you play a sport?
What sports do you enjoy playing most?
Who are your favourite sportspeople?

Are you interested in music?
What kinds of music do you like?

What hobbies do you have?
Do you collect anything?
Do you belong to any clubs?

Do you like reading?
What kinds of books and magazines do you read?

2 Class activity

Now compare your information. What do other people like?

3 Listening

1 Listen to four people talking. What are they talking about? Write the subject.

a .... b............................. c .... d ....

2 Now listen again. What was each person's reaction? Tick the correct response.

a .... She is confused.   c .... He couldn't understand it.
     .... She is afraid.   .... He thought it was very interesting.

b .... She enjoyed it.   d .... She thought it was all right.
     .... She hated it.   .... She thought it was terrible.

4   The best intentions ...

1   Pair work

What are some of the things you intend to do
in the near future? Think of three things.

I'm going to do more exercise.
I'm going to learn to play the guitar.

2   Class activity

Now go around the class and talk to three other students. Has anyone got the same
intentions as you? Then report the most interesting intention you heard.

Chris said he was going to learn to cook.
Eva said she was planning to get married in Hawaii.

5   What a chance!

1   Think of what you would do in these situations.

a If I had £1 000 to spend, I would …
b If I could invite anyone I wanted to dinner, …
c If I could have a holiday anywhere in the world, …
d If I could be Prime Minister for one day, …
e If I could be a famous person, …

2   Group work

Now compare your answers.

6   What's the joke?

1   Pair work

Look at these cartoons.

What are they about?
Do you think they are funny?
Why or why not?

2   Class activity

Compare your reactions
with other students.

'When you said you'd invited the family,
I didn't realise you meant *all* of them!'

'I can see why you told me it
was an unspoilt island!'

'Why ever did you say you wanted
this year's favourite breed?'

Interchange Activities

Interchange 1 Class profile

1 Class activity

Find out which people in the class have done the things below. When someone answers 'Yes', write down her/his name. Then ask another person the next question. Ask questions like this.

Did you use to have long hair?
Did you have a pet when you were a child?
Were you born more than 500 miles from here?

Find someone who …   Names

a used to have long hair.   ....

b had a pet when she/he was a child.   ....

c was born more than 500 miles from here.   ....

d used to go jogging when she/he was younger.   ....

e went to primary and secondary school in her/his home town.   ....

f played football at school.   ....

g used to collect stamps.   ....

h used to have a part-time job.   ....

i used to play the piano.   ....

2 Pair work

Now compare your information.

Interchange 2 Excuse me, I'm lost! – STUDENT A

1 Ask your partner how to get to the places below. Then mark them on your map.

the tourist office
the department store
the car park
the fish and chip shop
the launderette
the garage

2 Now use your map and give your partner the information she/he asks for.

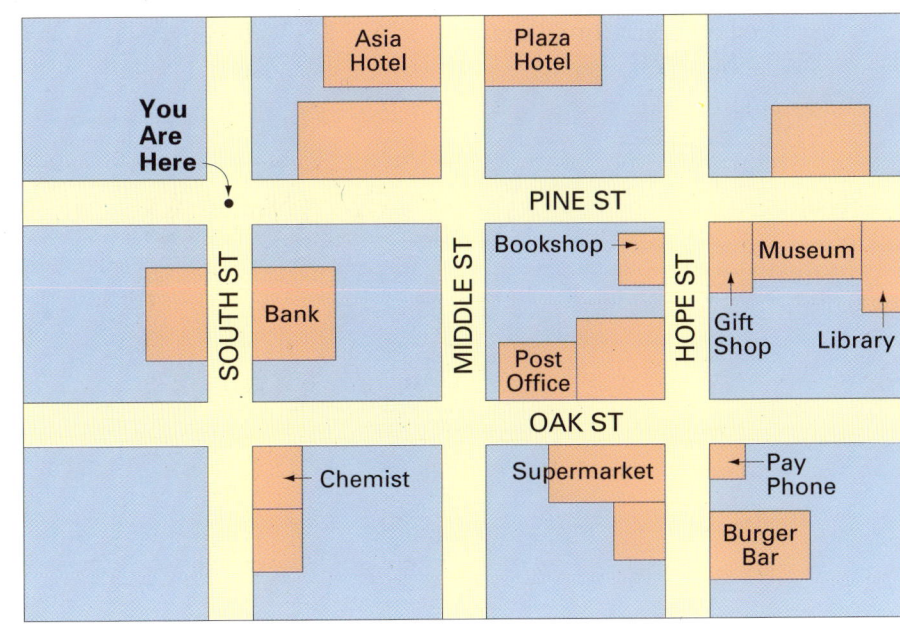

Interchange 2 Excuse me, I'm lost! – STUDENT B

1 Use your map and give your partner the information she/he asks for.

2 Now ask your partner how to get to the places below. Then mark them on your map.

the Plaza Hotel
the bookshop
the library
Burger Bar
the gift shop
the pay phone

Interchange 4 Their secret pasts!

1 **Class activity**

How much do you really know about other students in your class? Look at these lists and add two more things to ask to each list. Then go round the class and ask questions. Write down the names of people who answer 'Yes' for Part (a) and 'No' for Part (b). Ask like this.

Have you ever owned a motorbike?
Have you ever been to a beach party?

a Find two people who have …
   owned a motorbike.
   been to a beach party.
   cried during a film.
   studied all night for an exam.
   lied about their age.

   ....
   ....

Names
   ....
   ....
   ....
   ....
   ....
   ....
   ....

b Find two people who have never …
   eaten a curry.
   seen a wild animal.
   been camping.
   driven a car.
   seen a ballet.

   ....
   ....

Names
   ....
   ....
   ....
   ....
   ....
   ....
   ....

2 Do any names appear on both lists?

Interchange 3 Housing Survey

1 Pair work

Take turns. Use the questionnaire below and find out about your partner's home and neighbourhood.

---

a   What kind of accommodation do you live in?

☐ flat   ☐ house   ☐ other ....

b   How long have you been living there? Since .... (month/year)

c   How far is it from school? About .... (distance)

d   How many rooms has it got? ....

e   Has it got ...?

☐ central heating   ☐ a microwave   ☐ air conditioning   ☐ a garage

☐ a dishwasher   ☐ a garden   ☐ a washing machine   ☐ a good view

f   Are there any ... near you?

☐ restaurants   ☐ shops   ☐ supermarkets   ☐ cafés

☐ cinemas   ☐ parks   ☐ sports facilities   ☐ schools

g   Is your neighbourhood ...?

☐ crowded   ☐ clean   ☐ safe   ☐ quiet

---

2 Class activity

Now use the questionnaire and report your information to the class.

How many students ...

- live in flats?
- live in houses?
- live close to school?
- live more than five miles from school?
- have sports facilities near their houses?
- live in quiet neighbourhoods?

Interchange 5 Coastal fling – STUDENT A

1   Role play

You are in a travel agency reading about these trips to the United States, but you are not sure which one is better for you.

This is your chance ★ to see the U.S.

Choose a coast and have the holiday of your life! Prices from $1200 (not including airfare)

21-day East Coast Tour

See three historic cities in the US. Special winter rates. Deluxe hotel accommodation. Fantastic boat tour available.

15-day West Coast Tour

Visit three exciting cities! Tour available all year round. Single or double rooms. Special harbour cruise.

Talk to the travel agent and get more information. Start like this.
I want to take a trip to the US. Can you tell me about these tours?

Which cities will I visit on the East Coast/West Coast tour?
What kind of things can I do in … (name of city)?
I want to go in winter/summer. What's the weather like then?
What else can I see on the East Coast/West Coast tour?

Then tell the travel agent which tour you want to take and why.

2   Now change roles and partners. Look at page 130.

Interchange 6 That's no excuse! – STUDENT A

1 Role play

Read each situation below and then make a complaint to your partner. Use your own words and use your imagination! Your partner will give excuses.

a Your partner borrowed your favourite record two weeks ago. You'd like to have it back.

b Your partner promised to meet you at the cinema last night. You waited in front of the Cinerama Theatre but your friend never showed up. Finally you went in and saw the film alone.

2 Change partners. Now it's your turn to give excuses to your partner's complaints.

a Your neighbour is complaining about your dog. Apologise and promise you'll try to keep 'Bonzo' quiet and inside at nights.

b Your flatmate is complaining that her/his box of chocolates is empty. Explain that two friends came over and ate all of them. You couldn't stop them. Apologise and offer to buy your flatmate a new box tomorrow.

Interchange 5 Coastal fling – STUDENT B

1 Role play

You are a travel agent. A customer is asking you questions about these two trips to the United States. Use the information below to answer her/his questions.

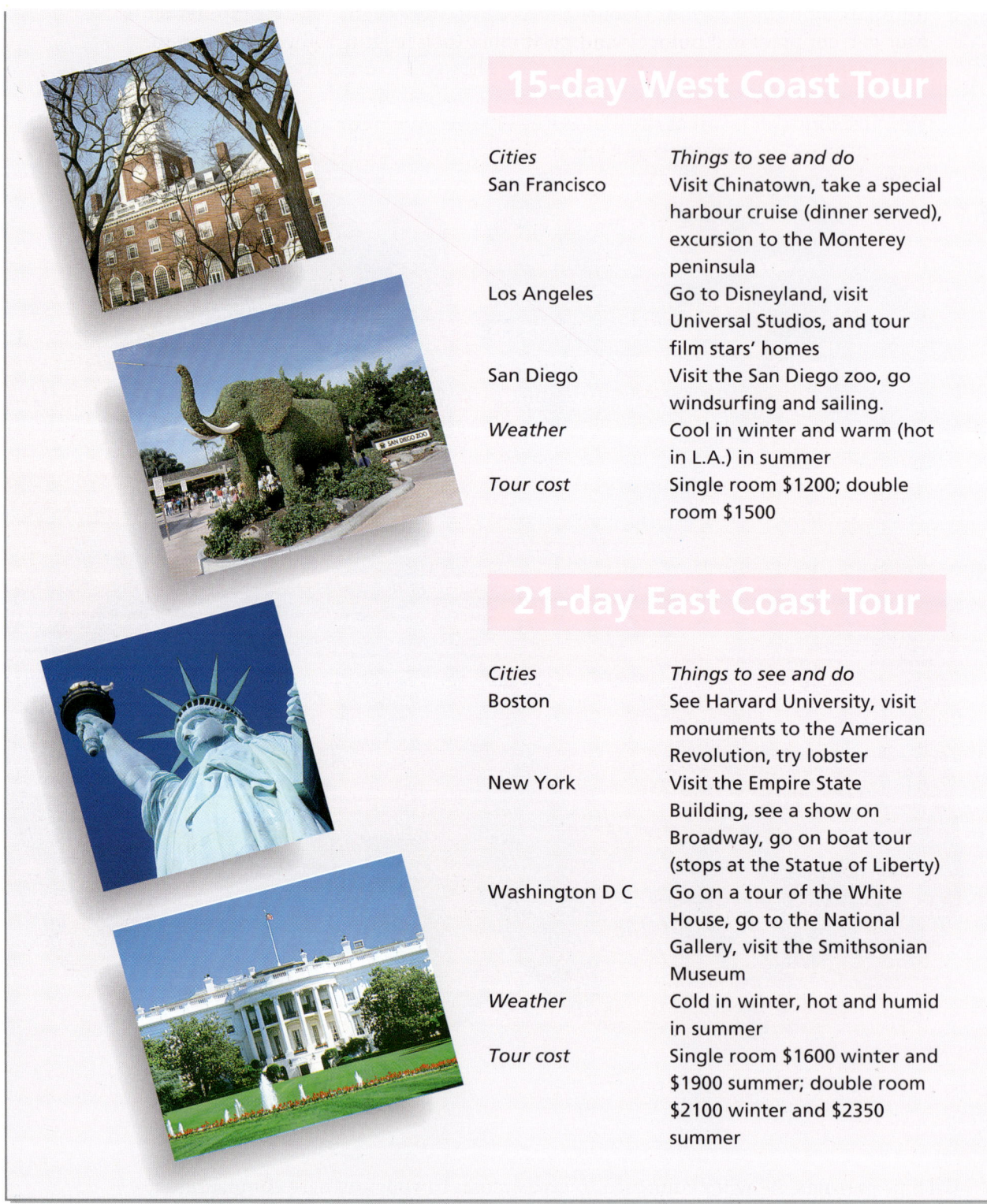

15-day West Coast Tour

Cities	Things to see and do
San Francisco	Visit Chinatown, take a special harbour cruise (dinner served), excursion to the Monterey peninsula
Los Angeles	Go to Disneyland, visit Universal Studios, and tour film stars' homes
San Diego	Visit the San Diego zoo, go windsurfing and sailing.
Weather	Cool in winter and warm (hot in L.A.) in summer
Tour cost	Single room $1200; double room $1500

21-day East Coast Tour

Cities	Things to see and do
Boston	See Harvard University, visit monuments to the American Revolution, try lobster
New York	Visit the Empire State Building, see a show on Broadway, go on boat tour (stops at the Statue of Liberty)
Washington D C	Go on a tour of the White House, go to the National Gallery, visit the Smithsonian Museum
Weather	Cold in winter, hot and humid in summer
Tour cost	Single room $1600 winter and $1900 summer; double room $2100 winter and $2350 summer

Then ask the customer if there is anything else she/he wants to do there. Finally ask which tour she/he wants to take.

2 Now change roles and partners. Look at page 128.

Interchange 6 That's no excuse! – STUDENT B

1 Role play

Read each situation below. Listen to your partner's complaints and then apologise and give an excuse. Use your own words and use your imagination!

a You borrowed your partner's favourite record two weeks ago. You want to return it but you can't find it. Apologise and promise to look for it tonight and return it as soon as possible.

b You promised to meet your partner at the cinema last night. Your partner complains that you didn't show up at the Cinerama Theatre. Apologise and explain that you thought you were going to the Odeon. You waited at the Odeon for an hour before going home.

2 Change partners. Now it's your turn to make complaints about these situations.

a Your neighbour has a large dog. The dog barks all night and keeps you awake. It also comes into your garden and chases your cat.

b You got a big box of your favourite chocolates for your birthday. When you returned home from school, there were no chocolates left in the box. You are sure your flatmate ate all of them.

Interchange 7 But it's almost new! – STUDENT A

Role play

a You are a sales assistant. A customer comes in. The customer has a problem with a video camera. You start. Begin like this:

'Yes, may I help you?'

 – Ask if the customer has checked the batteries.
 – Give another suggestion for the problem
   (e.g., the switches need to be repaired; the whole camera needs checking).
 – Ask the customer to leave the camera with you.
 – Arrange a day and time when the customer can pick it up.

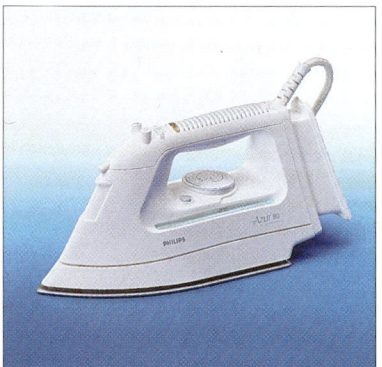

b You work in a shop. A customer brings back something she/he has bought.
   There is a problem with it.

 – Suggest what the problem might be.
 – Say that it needs to be repaired (or give another suitable explanation).
 – Ask the customer to leave the item with you. Say when it can be picked up.

c This time imagine you have bought something, but now you have a problem with it.
   Take it back to the shop and say what is wrong with it.
   The assistant will give you suggestions.

Interchange 8 Once in a blue moon

1 Class activity

How do other students in the class and the teacher celebrate special days and times? Go around the class and ask the questions below. If someone answers 'Yes' write down her/his name and ask for more information.

a Does your family often have big get-togethers?   ....
b Do you ever buy flowers for someone special?   ....
c Do you often take friends out for dinner?   ....
d Do you ever wear national dress?   ....
e Has anyone given you money recently as a gift?   ....
f Have you given money to anyone recently as a gift?   ....
g Do you often celebrate your birthday with a party?   ....
h Do you ever send birthday cards?   ....
i Do you ever give friends birthday presents?   ....
j Do you think long engagements are a good idea?   ....
k Is New Year your favourite time of the year?   ....
l Do you ever celebrate a holiday with fireworks?   ....

2 Pair work

Now compare your information.

Interchange 9 Pros and cons

1 Read these questions about controversial suggestions and add two more of your own. Then find out other students' opinions. Ask two students each question and tick the columns.

A: Do you think it is a good idea to tax drivers by the number of miles they drive? Why or why not?
B: Yes, because it's fairer to people who don't drive much.
C: No, because some people depend on their cars for work and it would be too expensive.

Do you think it is a good idea to …? Why or why not?	For	Against
a tax drivers by the number of miles they drive?	....	....
b reduce the working week to four days for all workers?	....	....
c allow people to use their cars only two days a week?	....	....
d require fifty percent of all government employees to be women?	....	....
e ban the sale of all products made of fur?	....	....
f make everyone give one day a month to community service?	....	....
g make bicycle riders wear helmets?	....	....
h ....?	....	....
i ....?	....	....

2 Class activity

How many students responded 'for' and 'against' to each question?
Which ideas were most popular?

Interchange 7 But it's almost new! – STUDENT B

Role play

a You bought a video camera recently, but it doesn't work. You take it back to the shop. Your partner starts.

  – Explain the problem.
  – You have already checked the batteries. They are OK.
  – The sales assistant suggests what is wrong. Agree with the sales assistant.
  – The sales assistant will ask you to leave the camera for repair. You agree.
  – Arrange a convenient day and time to pick it up.

b Imagine you have bought something recently but now you have a problem with it. Take it back to the shop and say what is wrong with it. The sales assistant will give you suggestions.

c This time you work in a shop. A customer brings back something she/he has bought. There is a problem with it.

  – Suggest what the problem might be.
  – Say that it needs to be repaired (or give another suitable explanation).
  – Ask the customer to leave the item with you. Say when it can be picked up.

Interchange 10 Nine to five

1   Write one or two sentences about yourself, describing

    a   your school life or your work experience;
    b   something you are good at doing and not so good at;
    or
    c   the kind of things you like doing and don't like doing.

The teacher will collect the information and put it on a class chart like this.

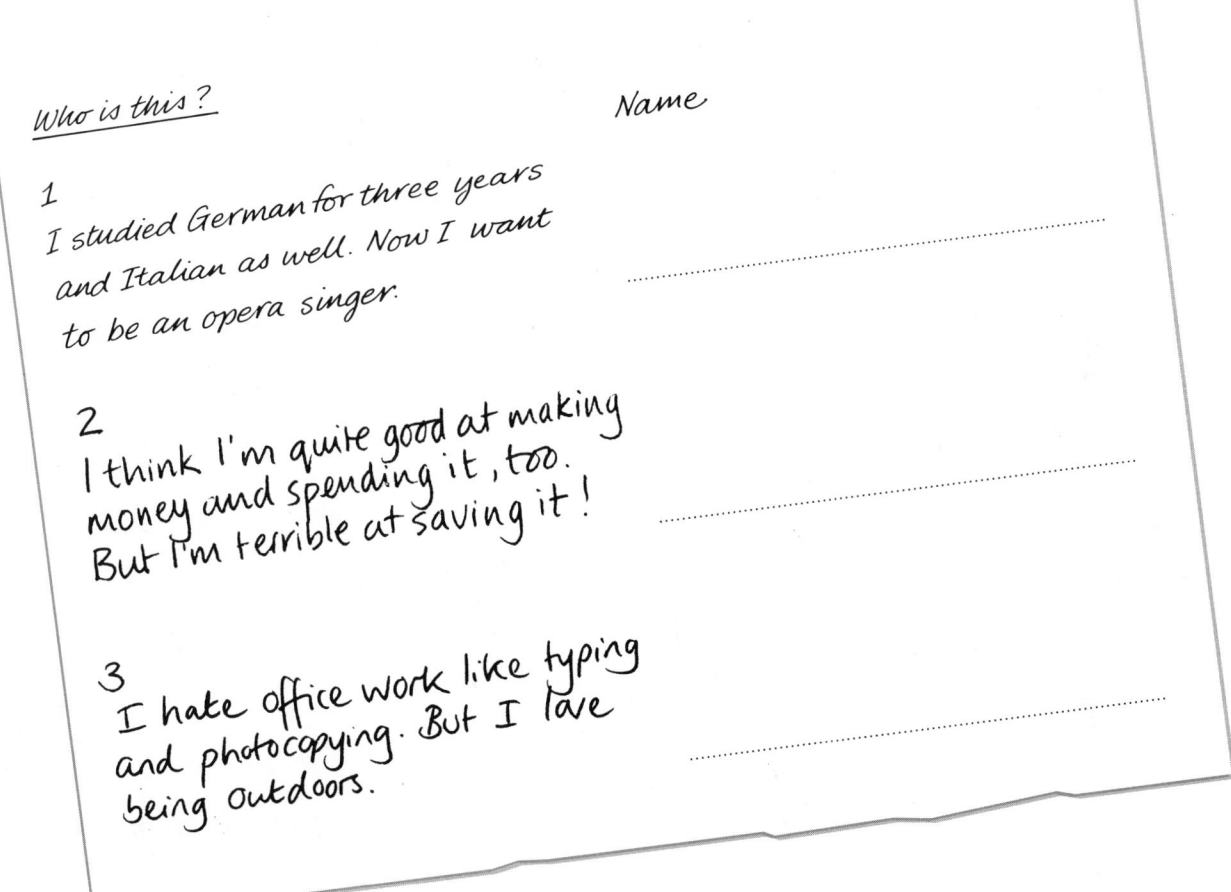

Who is this?   Name

1   I studied German for three years and Italian as well. Now I want to be an opera singer.

2   I think I'm quite good at making money and spending it, too. But I'm terrible at saving it!

3   I hate office work like typing and photocopying. But I love being outdoors.

2   **Class activity**

Now try to find which student wrote each piece of information. Ask questions like these.

Did you study German and Italian?
or
Do you want to be an opera singer?

Are you quite good at making money and spending it, too?
or
Do you have trouble saving money?

When you find the correct person, write her/his name on the chart.
Stop after ten minutes. How many names do you have?

Interchange 11 Culture quiz – GROUP A

1   Look at these questions and then add two more questions of your own to each category.

1 Music
a   Who is Robert Zimmerman?   (Bob Dylan)
b   What instrument did Louis Armstrong play?   (trumpet)
c   ....
d   ....

2 Films
a   Who was the film *ET* directed by?   (Steven Spielberg)
b   Who played the Joker in *Batman* (1989)?   (Jack Nicholson)
c   ....
d   ....

Guernica, 1937, by Pablo Picasso

3 Literature
a   Who was the play *Hamlet* written by?   (Shakespeare)
b   Who was the book *Frankenstein* written by? (Mary Shelley)
c   ....
d   ....

4 Art
a   Who was the picture *Guernica* painted by? (Picasso)
b   Who was the statue *David* made by?   (Michelangelo)
c   ....
d   ....

2   Now take turns asking Group B your questions. Which group got most correct answers?

Interchange 12 The Roving Reporter – STUDENT A

1   Role play

Imagine you are Michael J. Fox, the famous actor. You are going to be interviewed by The Roving Reporter. Use the information below to help you answer some of the Reporter's questions about your life. Make up answers of your own if necessary.

Michael J. Fox

- – born in Edmonton, Canada, on June 9th, 1961
- – father is a retired police officer
- – mother is an accounts clerk
- – moved to Vancouver at age 5
- – studied drama at school and acted in several plays
- – in 1978, worked in a Canadian TV comedy series
- – left school in 1979
- – moved to Los Angeles at age 19
- – acted in some films
- – in 1982 got a leading part in the TV series *Family Ties*
- – made several successful films:
  Back to the Future (1985)
  Secret of my Success (1987)
  Bright Lights, Big City (1988)
  Casualties of War (1989)
  Back to the Future Part 2 (1989)
  Back to the Future Part 3 (1990)

2

Now change partners and roles. You are the Roving Reporter. You are going to interview the famous singer Whitney Houston. Ask the following questions and some questions of your own.

When were you born?
Does your mother sing, too?
Where did you begin singing?
What other jobs have you done?
What was your first solo album?
Was it a success?
Do you have any interests outside singing?
Do you have a degree?
Are you married?
Do you have any children?
What have you been doing recently?

Interchange 11 Culture quiz – GROUP B

1 Look at these questions and then add two more questions to each category.

1 Music
a Who was the song *Material Girl* sung by?   (Madonna)
b What instrument did Ringo Starr play?   (drums)
c ....
d ....

2 Films
a Which actor played Rambo?   (Sylvester Stallone)
b Which actress is as famous for her marriage to
Richard Burton as she is for her film roles?   (Elizabeth Taylor)
c ....
d ....

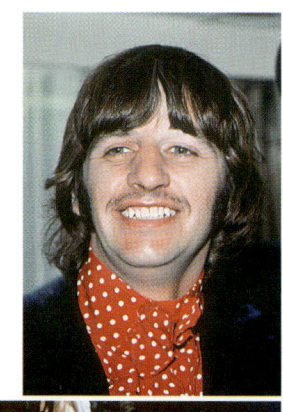

3 Literature
a Who was the mystery *Murder on the Orient Express* written by?   (Agatha Christie)
b Who was *The Adventures of Tintin* written by?   (Hergé)
c ....
d ....

4 Art
a Who was Mickey Mouse created by?   (Walt Disney)
b Who was the sculpture *The Thinker* made by?   (Auguste Rodin)
c ....
d ....

2 Now take turns asking Group A your questions. Which group got most correct answers?

Interchange 12 The Roving Reporter – STUDENT B

1 Role play

Imagine you are The Roving Reporter. You are going to interview the famous actor,
Michael J. Fox. Ask the following questions and some questions of your own.

Where were you born?   When did you move to Los Angeles?
What do your parents do?   Did you make any films in Hollywood before *Family Ties*?
Where did you live as a child?   Which of your films do you like the best?
Did you study acting at school?   What else have you been doing recently?
What did you do after that?

2

Now change partners and roles. Imagine you are Whitney Houston, the famous singer.
You are going to be interviewed by the Roving Reporter. Use the information below
to help you answer some of the reporter's questions about your life. Make up answers
of your own if necessary.

Whitney Houston

– born on August 9th, 1963, in Newark, New Jersey
– started singing in the New Hope Baptist Junior Choir where her
  mother, Cissy, was a Minister of Music
– at 15, was backing singer for Chaka Khan, Lou Rawls and for her
  mother's concert performances
– at 16, began modelling for magazine covers
– first album *Whitney Houston* went to number 1 and is the best
  selling album of all time by a solo performer
– in 1989, established The Whitney Houston Foundation for Children
  to help children in need
– works for other charities including the United Negro College Fund
  (UNCF), the American Red Cross and AIDS research
– in 1991, received an honorary
  doctorate in Humanities from
  Grambling University in Louisiana
– married singer Bobby Brown in 1992
– daughter Bobbi Kristina Brown
  born in March 1993
– started film career,
  co-starring with Kevin Costner
  in *The Bodyguard*

Interchange 13 Film Trivia

1   Group work

Take turns answering the questions below about films. Then compare your answers round the class. (Answers on page 142.)

a What famous film was about a huge shark?
b Can you name two films that Dustin Hoffman was in?
c Which famous director made *The Producers, Blazing Saddles, Silent Movie* and *High Anxiety*?
d Who directed and starred in *Dances with Wolves* in 1990?
e Can you name two films directed by Alfred Hitchcock?
f Which famous Swedish actress, who wanted to be alone, died in New York in 1990?
g Name an actor who has played the part of James Bond.
h Which actress won awards for *Taxi Driver* and *Bugsy Malone* in 1976 when she was fourteen?
i Can you name two films that Tom Cruise has been in?
j Name the famous black and white film about a gorilla that climbed the Empire State Building in New York.

2   Group work

Now make up your own Film Trivia quiz with ten questions like the ones above.

3   Class activity

Groups take turns asking their questions. The group with the most correct answers is the winner.

Interchange 14 Who said that?

1   Class activity

Go round the class and ask these questions. Fill in the chart.

	Name	Answer
a What's your favourite day of the year?	....	....
b What day of the week do you hate most?	....	....
c Which household job do you dislike most?	....	....
d What is one thing that other people do that makes you really angry?	....	....
e If you could change one thing in the world today, what would it be?	....	....
f What would you really like to get as a present?	....	....
g If you could live anywhere in the world where would you live?	....	....
h What is the best thing that has happened to you in the last month?	....	....
i If you could marry someone famous, who would it be?	....	....

2   Pair work

Now compare the answers you got.

Interchange 15 What would you have done?

1 Look at the situations below. What would you have done? Circle a, b, or c.

   1 An assistant in a shop gave you £10 extra change by mistake. Would you have …

     a returned the money?   b said nothing and kept it?   c given the money to charity?

   2 Another student cheated in an exam. Would you have …

     a done nothing?   b talked to the student?   c talked to the teacher?

   3 A friend painted a picture which you thought was awful. Would you have …

     a said something nice about it?   b said you didn't like it?   c said nothing?

   4 You were a guest in someone's house and were offered food that you didn't like.
Would you have …

     a said you weren't hungry?   b eaten the food?   c said, 'I don't really like this'?

2 Now interview other students in the class. What would they have said?
Do you agree? Start like this.

   A: What would you have done for number 1?
   B: Well, I probably would have …

3 **Pair work**

Read this predicament.

Tina and Rob were just finishing dinner on Saturday when the
doorbell rang. It was their good friends Cindy and Chris.
They thought they had been invited to a dinner party that
evening but they had made a mistake.
The dinner party was the next week.

If you had been Tina or Rob,
what would you have done?
Tell your partner. What would
you have done if you had
been Cindy or Chris?

4 **Pair work**

Now make up your own predicament. Tell your partner your predicament and ask
what she/he would have done.

Answers to Unit 11, Exercise 10.1

a in South America   b French and Flemish   c Indonesia and Malaysia
d Belgium, Canada, France, Haiti, Luxembourg, Morocco, Senegal, Switzerland, Tunisia, among other countries
e Australia, Canada, Denmark, Italy, Great Britain, Japan, Malaysia, the Netherlands, Norway, Portugal, Spain, Sweden, among other countries.

Answers to Units 10–12 Review, Exercise 6

1 Tina Turner;   2 Elizabeth Taylor;   3 Pavarotti;   4 John Lennon;   5 Mozart;   6 Julia Roberts

Answers to Interchange 13

a *Jaws*
b *Family Business, Rain Man, Tootsie, Kramer versus Kramer, The Graduate, Midnight Cowboy*, among others
c Mel Brooks
d Kevin Costner
e *The Birds, Dial M for Murder, North by Northwest, Notorious, Psycho, Rear Window, Strangers on a Train, Suspicion*, among others
f Greta Garbo   g Sean Connery, Roger Moore, Timothy Dalton   h Jodie Foster
i *Risky Business, Top Gun, The Color of Money, Rain Man, Born on the 4th July, Days of Thunder*
j *King Kong*

Irregular verbs

Present	Past	Participle	Present	Past	Participle
be: am/is, are	was, were	been	keep	kept	kept
bet	bet	bet	know	knew	known
blow	blew	blown	leave	left	left
break	broke	broken	lend	lent	lent
bring	brought	brought	lose	lost	lost
build	built	built	make	made	made
buy	bought	bought	mean	meant	meant
catch	caught	caught	meet	met	met
choose	chose	chosen	put	put	put
come	came	come	run	ran	ran
cost	cost	cost	say	said	said
cut	cut	cut	see	saw	seen
do	did	done	sell	sold	sold
drive	drove	driven	send	sent	sent
eat	ate	eaten	show	showed	shown
feel	felt	felt	sit	sat	sat
fight	fought	fought	speak	spoke	spoken
find	found	found	spend	spent	spent
fly	flew	flown	spread	spread	spread
forget	forgot	forgotten	stand	stood	stood
get	got	got	steal	stole	stolen
give	gave	given	stick	stuck	stuck
go	went	been/gone	swim	swam	swum
grow	grew	grown	take	took	taken
hang	hung/hanged	hung/hanged	tell	told	told
have	had	had	wear	wore	worn
hear	heard	heard	win	won	won
hide	hid	hidden	write	wrote	written
hold	held	held			

Tenses and verb forms

Present and past tenses

Present simple	I **live** in London.
Present continuous	I **am living** in London.
Present perfect	I **have lived** in London for two years.
Present perfect continuous	I **have been living** in London for two years.
Past simple	I **lived** in London two years ago.
Past continuous	I **was living** in London two years ago.
Past perfect	I **had worked** there for two years.
Past perfect continuous	I **had been working** there for two years.

Describing the future

With present simple	I **leave** tomorrow.
With present continuous	I **am leaving** tomorrow.
With *going to*	I **am going to leave** tomorrow.
With *will*	I **will leave** tomorrow.

Comparative and superlative adjectives

1 Adjectives with *-er* and *-est* (e.g., angry, angri**er**, angri**est**)

angry	cool	healthy	lovely	safe	strong
big	dirty	hot	mad	shy	warm
busy	fast	large	near	silly	weird
cheap	friendly	late	nice	small	wet
clean	funny	long	odd	steep	
cold	great	loud	old	strange	

2 Adjectives with *more* and *most* (e.g., dangerous, **more** dangerous, **most** dangerous)

amazing	dreadful	magnificent	slippery
awful	easygoing	modern	sociable
bad-tempered	exciting	pathetic	special
beautiful	expensive	patient	stupid
boring	fascinating	polite	successful
comfortable	forgetful	polluted	surprising
commercial	generous	prejudiced	talkative
confusing	hardworking	reasonable	terrible
creative	helpful	regular	terrific
crowded	horrible	reliable	useful
dangerous	impatient	religious	useless
delicious	intelligent	ridiculous	valuable
disgusting	interesting	serious	wonderful

3 Irregular adjectives

good	better	best
bad	worse	worst

Acknowledgements

Authors' acknowledgements
The authors would like to thank our editors at Cambridge University Press, Peter Donovan and Alison Sharpe, as well as Louise Elkins, Sini Haines and Louise Woods who provided invaluable suggestions during the preparation of *Changes*.

The authors and publishers are grateful to the following illustrators and photographic sources:
Kathy Baxendale, pp.17, 22, 24, 44, 84, 86, 101, 110, 125, 126; Peter Byatt, pp. 21, 60; David Downton, pp. 11, 18, 36, 41, 45, 50, 54, 57, 59, 70, 79, 82, 89, 94, 113, 117, 120; Martin Fish, p.124; Sue Hillwood Harris, pp. 20, 24, 33, 49, 56, 72, 82, 96, 100, 111, 118, 129, 131; Conny Jude, pp. 10, 19, 35, 41, 48, 55, 65, 73, 78, 80, 89, 93, 116, 141; Joanna Kerr, pp. 13, 17, 26, 33, 40, 50, 56, 63, 70, 79, 86, 95, 102, 109, 116; Brian Smith, pp. 47, 95; Julia Whatley, p.114; Kathy Wyatt, pp. 37, 44, 51, 66, 109

Photographers/Photographic sources:
Ace Photo Agency, pp. 26 (above left), 59 (above left), 138 (below right); Adams Picture Library, p. 43; Apple Computers Limited, pp. 77 (below right), 132 (below left); Art Directors Photo Library, p. 91 (below right); Aspect Picture Library Limited, p. 87; Barnaby's Picture Library, pp. 32 (above), 66 (right); © BBC, p. 105 (above); Musee Rodin, Paris/Bridgeman Art Library, London, p. 138 (above left), National Gallery, London/Bridgeman, p. 88 (above), Prado, Madrid/Bridgeman, p. 136 (above right); Britstock-IFA Limited/R Maier, p. 75 (above right), Britstock-IFA Limited/Erich Bach, p. 71 (right); BT Mobile, p. 132 (below centre); Camera Press Limited, pp. 97 (above right), 138 (above right); The J. Allan Cash Photolibrary, pp. 22 (above and below), 26 (right), 29 (above), 75 (above left), 91 (above right); Casio Electronics Company Limited, p. 134 (above right); © 1994 Comstock, Inc., p. 28 (above); Contiki Travel (UK) Limited, p. 42; Cresta Holidays, p. 42; Czech News Agency, p. 68 (centre); © DACS 1994, p.136 (above right); James Davis Travel Photography, pp. 90 (left), 130 (below); E.I. Company Limited, Ireland, p. 58 (below left); Greg Evans International, pp. 34, 65 (centre), 71 (centre), 75 (below centre), 81 (above right), 103; Chris Fairclough Colour Library, pp. 31 (above), 32 (below), 59 (below), 66 (left), 86; The Ronald Grant Archive, pp. 102, 107 (below), 138 (below centre); Sally and Richard Greenhill, pp. 10, 78, 81 (below); Robert Harding Picture Library, pp. 64 (below), 65 (above), 72 (above), 130 (above); Hitachi Sales Limited, p. 134 (centre left); Hoseasons Holidays Ltd; p.42; Hulton Deutsch Collection Limited, pp. 31 (upper centre, lower centre, below), 71 (left), 72 (below), Hulton/Syndication International, pp. 12, 15, 137; The Hutchison Library, pp. 67 (above left), 75 (below); Images Colour Library Limited, pp. 65 (below), 68 (above); Inspirations East Ltd., p.42; Columbia/Courtesy Kobal, pp. 13 (above), 107 (above), MGM/Pathe/Courtesy Kobal, p. 105 (below); Kumuka Expeditions, p.42; Moviestore Collection Limited, pp. 13 (below), 106 (above); Panasonic Consumer Electronics, p. 77 (centre); Pentax U.K. Limited, p. 77 (below left); Phillips Domestic Appliances, p. 132 (above right); Pictor International, pp. 88 (centre right), 121; Redferns, p. 136 (below centre); Retna Pictures Limited, p. 98, Retna/David Corio, p. 128 (left); Rex Features Limited, pp. 68 (below), 97 (above left), 97 (below left), 136 (below right), 139; Roland UK Ltd. p.58; Rowenta (U.K.) Limited, p. 134 (below left, below centre, below right); Sharp Electronics U.K. Limited, p. 132 (centre left); The Slide File, p. 64 (above); Sony Consumer Products Company U.K., pp. 77 (above), 132 (above left), 132 (below right), 134 (above left); Sovereign Sailing, p. 42; Spectrum Colour Library, pp. 75 (upper centre), 130 (below centre); Sporting Pictures U.K. Limited, p.91 (below left); Stanley Tools, p. 58; Tony Stone Images, pp. 14 (left), 26 (below centre), 27 (left and right), 28 (below), 42 (centre and below), 55, 74, 81 (centre), 88 (centre left, below left), 90 (above right, below right), 91 (above left), 101 (right), 128 (right), 130 (above centre); Telegraph Colour Library, p.81 (above left), Telegraph/Colorific Photo Library, pp. 38 (below right), 67 (above right), 106 below) Titan Travel Ltd., p.42; Top Deck, p.42; Topham Picturepoint, pp. 29 (below), 67 (below right), 101 (left), 136 (above left); Trip/Helene Rogers, pp. 38 (below left), 59 (above right); Viewfinder Colour Photo Library, pp. 38 (above), 120; John Walmsley Photo Library, pp. 14 (right), 93; 'Waymaster' - A Kenwood Company, p. 58 (above left).

Photographs on pp. 42 (above), 57 (above, centre, below), by Graham Portlock.

Every endeavour has been made to contact copyright owners and apologies are expressed for any omissions.

Picture Research by Sandie Huskinson-Rolfe (PHOTOSEEKERS).

Design by Newton Harris.